THE POPULISTS IN HISTORICAL PERSPECTIVE

Problems in American Civilization

The POPULISTS

in HISTORICAL PERSPECTIVE

EDITED WITH AN INTRODUCTION BY

Raymond J. Cunningham

FORDHAM UNIVERSITY

D. C. HEATH AND COMPANY

A division of RAYTHEON EDUCATION COMPANY

LEXINGTON, MASSACHUSETTS

Library of Congress Catalog Card Number: 68-19012

INTRODUCTION

THE modern historiography of Populism falls naturally into three major divisions: the origins of the movement, the character of Populist ideology, and the role of the party in the campaign of 1896. Within these large categories a multitude of interpretations present themselves to the critical student. In offering the selections in this volume it is not the editor's expectation that the reader will be able to arrive at conclusive judgments regarding these various positions and emphases. Much more intensive inquiry is necessary before one might safely venture so far. Hopefully, the student will obtain a reasonably clear understanding of the problems involved in interpreting Populism and will perhaps be led to pursue these issues further.

During the years when Populism was a vital force in political life, American historical writing was still dominated by Eastern scholars whose economic and social attitudes were basically conservative. These historians seldom gave much attention to current agrarian unrest, but, when they did, they revealed their conservative Eastern bias by a condescending or openly hostile treatment. In these very years, however, the character of American historical scholarship was changing as young historians, particularly from the Midwest and South, began their careers. This younger generation, of which Frederick Jackson Turner is typical, upheld liberal values more sympathetic to agrarian protest than the conservatism of their predecessors. Because the thought and writing of these new men originated, in part, as a scholarly expression of emerging Progressivism, they and their successors have been aptly called the progressive school. For nearly a half century the monographic studies and comprehensive surveys by these scholars recast American history in the mold of twentieth-century liberalism, and the spirit of their work is by no means devoid of influence today. Thus, the contributions of three leading progressive historians represent not only the mainstream of Populist historiography, but also the larger liberal orientation of the progressive school.

It is appropriate that this volume open with an essay by Turner, written for the *Atlantic Monthly* in the midst of the 1896 campaign. The progressive historians were especially concerned with the origins of Populism, and Turner was particularly well suited to explain the background of this movement to the sophisticated Easterners toward whom this periodical was chiefly directed. Having taken his bachelor's and master's degrees at the University of Wisconsin, Turner became a student at Johns Hopkins University, then the most influential of the new American graduate schools established on the German model. Although he accepted the professional methodology of the Eastern institution, he resisted Professor Herbert Adams' explanation of American history as the evolution of Anglo-Saxon racial "germs" implanted in the New World by the early English settlers. Fully aware of America's European heritage, Turner nevertheless refused to see it as the determinative factor in shaping national character and institutions. Instead, he contended that "the existence of an area of free land, its continuous recession, and the advance of American settlement westward, explain American development." In the selection reprinted here the reader should note the extent to which Turner's "frontier thesis" underlies his explanation of agrarian unrest.

Two important studies written by Solon Buck in 1913 and 1920 on the "agrarian crusade" carried the progressive interpretative trend forward; they were confirmed in John D. Hicks's appreciative work, *The Populist Revolt* (1931). Hicks's study traces the Populist movement from its origins in the Farmers' Alliance through its rapid decline after 1896. Although his work remains the most comprehensive treatment of agrarian radicalism, recent critics have noted its limitations. Like Turner, Hicks was a Midwesterner who tended to overstress the role of his section while neglecting the Southern contribution to Populism. More important, in considering the agrarian revolt to be the precursor of twentieth-century reformism, he typified the progressive historians' simplistic conceptualization of modern American history as a sequence of closely related reform movements — Populism, Progressivism, and the New Deal. Yet Hicks's elucidation of the underlying economic grievances of the farmer, in the South as well as in the West, has not been substantially altered by later investigation, and his analysis, reprinted here, goes to the heart of any attempt to understand the origins of Populism.

Chester Destler's study of the origins of Western radicalism reveals the extent to which the progressive method of interpretation had permeated historical thought by the mid-1940's. Between the appearance of Hicks's volume and Destler's article, the United States had passed through the crucible of the Great Depression and the challenge of the New Deal. The spirit of reform and innovation characteristic of that era made a strong appeal to the scholarly community and

extended the influence of the progressive historical vision. No longer could it be said that the center of progressive historical writing lay in the West, for many leading progressive historians were Easterners teaching at Eastern universities. Not surprisingly, the progressivism of the Eastern scholars sometimes expressed a viewpoint different from that of their Western colleagues. For example, whereas Turner and Hicks stress the fact that agrarian radicalism arose out of specific Western (and, to a lesser extent, Southern) economic and political grievances, Destler suggests that the inspiration for many agrarian ideas and programs lay in the Eastern cities. One should examine the validity of Destler's contention on the basis of his evidence. But further, one should also inquire whether Destler disagrees with his Western predecessors in any fundamental way or whether his work simply offers new insights within the traditional progressive framework.

By the middle of the 1950's the long dominant progressive interpretation of Populism came under serious attack by a number of historians and social scientists. While these revisionist scholars represented a wide range of backgrounds and attitudes, they agreed that Populist ideology was less a realistic response to actual grievances than an irrational expression of fears and anxieties conjured up by the farmers' predicament. Of the revisionist studies appearing in these years, the section dealing with Populism in Richard Hofstadter's *The Age of Reform* (1955) was undoubtedly the most influential. Although some revisionists were conservative, Hofstadter's liberalism was more radical than that of the progressive historians. Hofstadter's disenchantment with Populism was part of his larger disenchantment with American reform which he found forever insufficient in its efforts at social reconstruction. Thus one of the most serious limitations of Populist thought, according to Hofstadter, was its essentially nostalgic character — its pre-industrial, backward-looking ideology. Expanding this thesis, he names five concepts as principal ingredients in "the folklore of Populism." This analysis should suggest many questions about Hofstadter's relation to earlier historians. Does he, for example, minimize the economic grievances which the progressive school found central to Populism? Does he deny completely the validity of the Populists' reform program?

Unlike the progressive interpretation, the revisionist view was quickly challenged by historians who were unconvinced by the revisionists and who sought to preserve the good repute of the Populist movement. Norman Pollack's closely reasoned essay focuses specifically on Hofstadter's treatment of Populism. Pollack rejects Hofstadter's "consensus thesis" and therefore rejects his entire interpretation of Populist protest as fundamentally irrational. Furthermore, Pollack is highly critical of Hofstadter's five themes and of the evidence adduced to support them. He also raises the important issue of the proper role of psychological analysis in history. However, it is possible to question Pollack's charge that Hofstadter's reasoning necessarily implies "a blanket endorsement of industrial capitalism and a consequent denial that conditions of oppression and concrete economic grievances existed."

Walter Nugent's study is not a direct rebuttal of Hofstadter, but a detailed analysis of Populist attitudes in Kansas, one of the most important centers of the movement. Like Pollack, he concentrates on the principal charges levelled against the Populist mentality by the revisionists,

and he concludes that, in Kansas at least, these charges are largely unfounded. Nugent sees the ideology of the Kansas Populists not as a mixture of irrational apprehension and hysterical rhetoric, but as a reasonable response to their economic plight. Although on the one hand Nugent is obviously at odds with the main thrust of revisionism, on the other hand he accepts in a very qualified manner a few revisionist opinions on Populist thought.

Of the criticisms of revisionism presented here, C. Vann Woodward's essay is most sympathetic to the revisionist point of view and most searching in its attempt to explain the rise of Populist revisionism. Here he attempts to account for the intellectuals' generally appreciative attitude toward Populism during the 1930's turning to antipathy in the 1940's and 1950's. An important feature of Woodward's defense of the Populist tradition is his demonstration that the farmers were not the only segment of the population influenced by myths and stereotypes. Woodward concentrates much of his attention on the Southern Populist experience, a facet often neglected by historians.

The most recent phase of the historiography of Populism deals with its role in the campaign of 1896. The traditional interpretation of this important episode in American political history is presented succinctly in a selection from Matthew Josephson's popular work, The Politicos (1938). According to this long held view, the decision reached at the St. Louis Populist convention to join with Bryan Democrats and to concentrate on the free silver issue constituted a betrayal of the ideals and interests of rank and file Populists by opportunistic party leaders. Robert F. Durden, recently reexamining this question, concludes that the position taken by Josephson and his supporters is not tenable. Durden contends that fusion was a hard-headed, responsible and widely-supported solution to the political situation confronting the Populists in 1896. The reader should not only note how Durden develops his case, but also why he rejects the traditional position.

If it is true that every man is his own historian, then on the basis of these readings the student may be expected to form his own tentative conclusions about the nature of Populism. In assessing the current status of a historical problem, one must, of course, be guided by factual evidence. But such assessments will also necessarily involve less tangible factors such as the value judgments of historians and, more recently, of social scientists.

The disagreements between progressives and revisionists, for example, are not essentially disagreements about the facts. They are differences about the character of Populist thought and the extent of Populist reform, and about the application of social science concepts to historical analysis. Likewise, evaluations of the course taken by the Populist Party in 1896 rest not only on the facts but also on historians' opinions about wise and responsible political behavior. The reader's assessment of the interpretations presented here will inevitably be conditioned by a similar combination of factual evidence and value judgment.

[Note: Footnotes have generally been omitted from the selections that follow, except where needed to explain the text.]

CONTENTS

A midwestern scholar, writing the standard history of Populism, explains:

> Beset on every hand by demands for funds . . . the farmer naturally enough raised the battle cry of "more money." . . . There must be something more fundamentally wrong than the misdeeds of railroads and trusts and tax assessors. Why should dollars grow dearer and dearer and scarcer and scarcer? Why, indeed, unless because of the manipulations of those to whom such a condition would bring profit?
>
> JOHN D. HICKS

While a leading revisionist historian writes:

> There is indeed much that is good and usable in our Populist past. . . . But anyone who enlarges our portrait of the Populist tradition is likely to bring out some unseen blemishes. In the books that have been written about the Populist movement, only passing mention has been made of its significant provincialism; little has been said of its relations with nativism and nationalism; nothing has been said of its tincture of anti-Semitism.
>
> RICHARD HOFSTADTER

But a careful critic of revisionism asserts:

> The Populists have been accused of nativism . . .; instead, they were friendlier and more receptive to foreign persons and foreign institutions than the average of their contemporary political opponents. They have been accused of "conspiracy-mindedness"; for them, however, tangible fact quite eclipsed neurotic fiction. They have been accused of anti-Semitism . . .; instead they consistently . . . refrained from extending their dislike of certain financiers, who happened to be Jews, to Jews in general.
>
> WALTER T. K. NUGENT

Explaining the Populist decision at the St. Louis convention to fuse with the Democrats in 1896, a historian expresses the traditional view:

> To St. Louis . . . the agents of the silver cabal quickly repaired, bent as they had been for two years on achieving fusion between the Populists and the Democrats. . . .
>
> These men now contrived to manage the Populist convention by means of wirepulling as effective as any party assembly ever saw. Henry Demarest Lloyd . . . reflected on how curious it was that ". . . the People's party, should be more boss-ridden, gang-ruled, gang-gangrened than the two old parties of monopoly."
>
> MATTHEW JOSEPHSON

But a more recent appraisal views the decision quite differently:

> Such a struggle as the Populists had waged at St. Louis left serious divisions in the party. Yet the important fact is that the great majority of the party and its leaders had held together for Bryan and national reforms. . . . Free silver, far from being a "cow-bird," had swept the Populists into an important role in the epochal campaign of 1896.
>
> ROBERT F. DURDEN

I. THE ORIGINS OF POPULISM: THE PROGRESSIVE SCHOOL

Frederick Jackson Turner: THE PROBLEM OF THE WEST

Frederick Jackson Turner was the first American historian to view Western development as the chief factor in shaping American history. Though a Westerner who generally celebrated Western traits, he was also a professional historian who had trained at Johns Hopkins University and who later taught at Harvard. He was, therefore, in an excellent position to interpret the West to the East. Here Turner attempts to do just this, giving particular attention to the Populist excitement then at its height.

THE PROBLEM of the West is nothing less than the problem of American development. A glance at the map of the United States reveals the truth. To write of a "Western sectionalism," bounded on the east by the Alleghanies, is, in itself, to proclaim the writer a provincial. What is the West? What has it been in American life? To have the answers to these questions, is to understand the most significant features of the United States of to-day.

The West, at bottom, is a form of society, rather than an area. It is the term applied to the region whose social conditions result from the application of older institutions and ideas to the transforming influences of free land. By this application, a new environment is suddenly entered, freedom of opportunity is opened, the cake of custom is broken, and new activities, new lines of growth, new institutions and new ideals, are brought into existence. The wilderness disappears, the "West" proper passes on to a new frontier, and, in the former area, a new society has emerged from this contact with the backwoods. Gradually this society loses its primitive conditions, and assimilates itself to the type of the older social conditions of the East; but it bears within it enduring and distinguishing survivals of its frontier experience. Decade after decade, West after West, this rebirth of American society has gone on, has left its traces behind it, and has reacted on the East. The history of our political institutions, our democracy, is not a history of imitation, of simple borrowing; it is a history of the evolution and adaptation of organs in response to changed environment, a history of the origin of new political species. In this sense, therefore, the West has been a constructive force of the highest significance in our life. . . .

The West, as a phase of social organization, began with the Atlantic coast, and passed across the continent. But the colonial tide-water area was in close touch with the Old World, and soon lost its Western aspects. In the middle of the eighteenth century, the newer social conditions appeared along the upper waters of the tributaries of the Atlantic. Here it was that the West took on its distinguishing features, and transmitted frontier

From Frederick Jackson Turner, "The Problem of the West," *The Atlantic Monthly: A Magazine of Literature, Science, Art, and Politics,* LXXVIII (Sept. 1896), pp. 289–297.

traits and ideals to this area in later days. On the coast were the fishermen and skippers, the merchants and planters, with eyes turned toward Europe. Beyond the falls of the rivers were the pioneer farmers, largely of non-English stock, Scotch-Irish and German. They constituted a distinct people, and may be regarded as an expansion of the social and economic life of the middle region into the back country of the South. These frontiersmen were the ancestors of Boone, Andrew Jackson, Calhoun, Clay, and Lincoln. Washington and Jefferson were profoundly affected by these frontier conditions. The forest clearings have been the seed plots of American character.

In the Revolutionary days, the settlers crossed the Alleghanies and put a barrier between them and the coast. They became, to use their phrases, "the men of the Western waters," the heirs of the "Western world." In this era, the backwoodsmen, all along the western slopes of the mountains, with a keen sense of the difference between them and the dwellers on the coast, demanded organization into independent States of the Union. Self-government was their ideal. Said one of their rude, but energetic petitions for statehood: "Some of our fellow-citizens may think we are not able to conduct our affairs and consult our interests; but if our society is rude, much wisdom is not necessary to supply our wants, and a fool can sometimes put on his clothes better than a wise man can do it for him." This forest philosophy is the philosophy of American democracy. But the men of the coast were not ready to admit its implications. They apportioned the state legislatures so that the property-holding minority of the tidewater lands were able to outvote the more populous back counties. A similar system was proposed by federalists in the Constitutional Convention of 1787. Gouverneur Morris, arguing in favor of basing representation on property as well as numbers, declared that "he looked forward, also, to that range of new States which would soon be formed in the West. He thought the rule of representation ought to be so fixed, as to secure to the Atlantic States a prevalence in the national councils." . . .

From the first, it was recognized that a new type was growing up beyond the mountains, and that the time would come when the destiny of the nation would be in Western hands. The divergence of these societies became clear in the struggle over the ratification of the federal constitution. The interior agricultural region, the communities that were in debt and desired paper money, opposed the instrument; but the areas of intercourse and property carried the day.

It is important to understand, therefore, what were some of the ideals of this early Western democracy. How did the frontiersman differ from the man of the coast?

The most obvious fact regarding the man of the Western waters is that he had placed himself under influences destructive to many of the gains of civilization. Remote from the opportunity for systematic education, substituting a log hut in the forest clearing for the social comforts of the town, he suffered hardships and privations, and reverted in many ways to primitive conditions of life. Engaged in a struggle to subdue the forest, working as an individual, and with little specie or capital, his interests were with the debtor class. At each stage of its advance, the West has favored an expansion of the currency. The pioneer had boundless confidence in the future of his own community, and when seasons of financial contraction and depression occurred, he, who had staked his all on confidence in Western development, and had fought the savage for his home, was inclined to reproach the conservative sections and classes. To explain this antagonism requires more than denunciation of dishonesty, ignorance, and boorishness as fundamental Western traits. Legislation in the United States has had to deal with two distinct social conditions. In some portions of the country there was, and is, an aggregation of property, and vested rights are in the foreground: in others, capital is lacking, more primitive conditions prevail, with different economic and social ideals, and the contentment of the average individual is placed in the foreground. That in the conflict between these two ideals an even hand has always been held by the government would be difficult to show.

The separation of the Western man from the seaboard, and his environment, made him in a large degree free from European precedents and forces. He looked at things independently and with small regard or appreciation for the best Old World experience. . . .

His was rather the ideal of conserving and developing what was original and valuable in this new country. The entrance of old society upon free lands meant to him opportunity for a new type of democracy and new popular ideals. The West was not conservative: buoyant self-confidence and self-assertion were distinguishing traits in its composition. It saw in its growth nothing less than a new order of society and state. In this conception were elements of evil and elements of good.

But the fundamental fact in regard to this new society was its relation to land. Professor Boutmy has said of the United States, "Their one primary and predominant object is to cultivate and settle these prairies, forests, and vast waste lands.

The striking and peculiar characteristic of American society is that it is not so much a democracy as a huge commercial company for the discovery, cultivation, and capitalization of its enormous territory. The United States are primarily a commercial society, and only secondarily a nation." Of course, this involves a serious misapprehension. By the very fact of the task here set forth, far-reaching ideals of the state and of society have been evolved in the West, accompanied by loyalty to the nation representative of these ideals. But M. Boutmy's description hits the substantial fact, that the fundamental traits of the man of the interior were due to the free lands of the West. These turned his attention to the great task of subduing them to the purposes of civilization, and to the task of advancing his economic and social status in the new democracy which he was helping to create. . . .

But free lands and the consciousness of working out their social destiny did more than turn the Westerner to material interests and devote him to a restless existence. They promoted equality among the Western settlers, and reacted as a check on the aristocratic influences of the East. Where everybody could have a farm, almost for taking it, economic equality easily resulted, and this involved political equality. Not without a struggle would the Western man abandon this ideal, and it goes far to explain the unrest in the remote West to-day. . . .

It followed from the lack of organized political life, from the atomic conditions of the backwoods society, that the individual was exalted and given free play. The West was another name for opportunity. Here were mines to be seized, fertile valleys to be preëmpted, all the natural resources open to the shrewdest and the boldest. The United States is unique in the extent to which the individual has been given an open field, unchecked by restraints of an old social order, or of scientific administration of government. The self-made man was the Western man's ideal, was the kind of man that all men might become. Out of his wilderness experience, out of the freedom of his opportunities, he fashioned a formula for social regeneration, — the freedom of the individual to seek his own. He did not consider that his conditions were exceptional and temporary. . . .

The Western man believed in the manifest destiny of his country. On his border, and checking his advance, were the Indian, the Spaniard, and the Englishman. He was indignant at Eastern indifference and lack of sympathy with his view of his relations to these peoples; at the short-sightedness of Eastern policy. The closure of the Mississippi by Spain, and the proposal to exchange our claim of freedom of navigating the river, in return for commercial advantages to New England, nearly led to the withdrawal of the West from the Union. It was the Western demands that brought about the purchase of Louisiana, and turned the scale in favor of declaring the War of 1812. Militant qualities were favored by the annual expansion of the settled area in the face of hostile Indians and the stubborn wilderness. . . .

In spite of his rude, gross nature, this early Western man was an idealist withal. He dreamed dreams and beheld visions. He had faith in man, hope for democracy, belief in America's destiny, unbounded confidence in his ability to make his dreams come true. . . .

It is important to bear this idealism of the West in mind. The very materialism that has been urged aganst the West was accompanied by ideals of equality, of the exaltation of the common man, of na-

tional expansion, that make it a profound mistake to write of the West as though it were engrossed in mere material ends. It has been, and is, preëminently a region of ideals, mistaken or not.

It is obvious that these economic and social conditions were so fundmental in Western life that they might well dominate whatever accessions came to the West by immigration from the coast sections or from Europe. Nevertheless, the West cannot be understood without bearing in mind the fact that it has received the great streams from the North and from the South, and that the Mississippi compelled these currents to intermingle. Here it was that sectionalism first gave way under the pressure of unification. Ultimately the conflicting ideas and institutions of the old sections struggled for dominance in this area under the influence of the forces that made for uniformity, but this is merely another phase of the truth that the West must become unified, that it could not rest in sectional groupings. For precisely this reason the struggle occurred. In the period from the Revolution to the close of the War of 1812, the democracy of the Southern and Middle States contributed the main streams of settlement and social influence to the West. Even in Ohio political power was soon lost by the New England leaders. The democratic spirit of the Middle region left an indelible impress on the West in this its formative period. After the War of 1812, New England, its supremacy in the carrying trade of the world having vanished, became a beehive from which swarms of settlers went out to western New York and the remoter regions. These settlers spread New England ideals of education and character and political institutions, and acted as a leaven of great significance in the Northwest. But it would be a mistake to believe that an unmixed New England influence took possession of the Northwest. These pioneers did not come from the class that conserved the type of New England civilization pure and undefiled. They represented a less contented, less conservative influence. Moreover, by their sojourn in the Middle region, on their westward march, they underwent modification, and when the farther West received them, they suffered a forest-change, indeed. The Westernized New England man was no longer the representative of the section that he left. He was less conservative, less provincial, more adaptable and approachable, less rigorous in his Puritan ideals, less a man of culture, more a man of action.

As might have been expected, therefore, the Western men, in the era of good feeling, had much homogeneity throughout the Mississippi valley, and began to stand as a new national type. Under the lead of Henry Clay they invoked the national government to break down the mountain barrier by internal improvements, and thus to give their crops an outlet to the coast. Under him they appealed to the national government for a protective tariff to create a home market. A group of frontier States entered the Union with democratic provisions respecting the suffrage, and with devotion to the nation that had given them their lands, built their roads and canals, regulated their territorial life, and made them equals in the sisterhood of States. At last these Western forces of aggressive nationalism and democracy took possession of the government in the person of the man who best embodied them, Andrew Jackson. . . .

The next phase of Western development revealed forces of division between the northern and southern portions of the West. With the spread of the cotton cul-

ture went the slave system and the great plantation. The small farmer in his log cabin, raising varied crops, was displaced by the planter raising cotton. In all except the mountainous areas, the industrial organization of the tidewater took possession of the Southwest, the unity of the back country was broken, and the solid South was formed. In the Northwest this was the era of railroads and canals, opening the region to the increasing stream of Middle State and New England settlement, and strengthening the opposition to slavery. A map showing the location of the men of New England ancestry in the Northwest would represent also the counties in which the Free Soil party cast its heaviest votes. The commercial connections of the Northwest likewise were reversed by the railroad. . . .

The West broke asunder, and the great struggle over the social system to be given to the lands beyond the Mississippi followed. In the Civil War the Northwest furnished the national hero — Lincoln was the very flower of frontier training and ideal — and it also took into its hands the whole power of the government. Before the war closed, the West could claim the President, Vice-President, Chief Justice, Speaker of the House, Secretary of the Treasury, Postmaster-General, Attorney-General, General of the army, and Admiral of the navy. The leading generals of the war had been furnished by the West. It was the region of action, and in the crisis it took the reins.

The triumph of the nation was followed by a new era of Western development. The national forces projected themselves across the prairies and plains. Railroads, fostered by government loans and land grants, opened the way for settlement and poured a flood of European immigrants and restless pioneers from all sections of the Union into the government lands. The army of the United States pushed back the Indian, rectangular Territories were carved into checkerboard States, creations of the federal government, without a history, without physiographical unity, without particularistic ideas. The later frontiersman leaned on the strong arm of national power.

At the same time the South underwent a revolution. The plantation, based on slavery, gave place to the farm, the gentry to the democratic elements. As in the West, new industries, of mining and of manufacture, sprang up as by magic. The New South, like the New West, was an area of construction, a debtor area, an area of unrest; and it, too, had learned the uses to which federal legislation might be put.

In the mean time the old Northwest has passed through an economic and social transformation. The whole West has furnished an area over which successive waves of economic development have passed. The Indian hunters and traders were followed by the pioneer farmers, engaged in raising unrotated crops; after this came the wave of more settled town life and varied agriculture; the wave of manufacture followed. These stages of development have passed in succession across large parts of the old Northwest. The State of Wisconsin, now much like parts of the State of New York, was at an earlier period like the State of Nebraska of to-day; the granger movement and the greenback party had for a time the ascendency; and in the northern counties of the State, where there is a sparser population, and the country is being settled, its sympathies are still with the debtor class. Thus the old Northwest is a region where the older frontier conditions survive in parts, and where the inherited ways of looking at things are

largely to be traced to its frontier days. At the same time it is a region in many ways assimilated to the East. It understands both sections. It is not entirely content with the existing structure of economic society in the sections where wealth has accumulated and corporate organizations are powerful; but neither has it seemed to feel that its interests lie in supporting the programme of the prairies and the South. In the Fifty-third Congress it voted for the income tax, but it rejected free coinage. It is still affected by the ideal of the self-made man, rather than by the ideal of industrial nationalism. It is more American, but less cosmopolitan than the seaboard.

We are now in a position to see clearly some of the factors involved in the Western problem. For nearly three centuries the dominant fact in American life has been expansion. With the settlement of . . . the free lands, this movement had come to a check. That these energies of expansion will no longer operate would be a rash prediction; and the demands for a vigorous foreign policy, for an interoceanic canal, for a revival of our power upon the seas, and for the extension of American influence to outlying islands and adjoining countries, are indications that the movement will continue. The stronghold of these demands lies west of the Alleghanies.

In the remoter West, the restless, rushing wave of settlement has broken with a shock against the arid plains. The free lands are gone, the continent is crossed, and all this push and energy is turning into channels of agitation. Failures in one area can no longer be made good by taking up land on a new frontier; the conditions of a settled society are being reached with suddenness and with confusion. The West has been built up with borrowed capital, and the question of the stability of gold, as a standard of deferred payments, is eagerly agitated by the debtor West, profoundly dissatisfied with the industrial conditions that confront it, and actuated by frontier directness and rigor in its remedies. For the most part, the men who built up the West beyond the Mississippi, and who are now leading the agitation, came as pioneers from the old Northwest, in the days when it was just passing from the stage of a frontier section. For example, Senator Allen of Nebraska, president of the recent national Populist Convention, and a type of the political leaders of his section, was born in Ohio in the middle of the century; went in his youth to Iowa, and not long after the Civil War made his home in Nebraska. As a boy, he saw the buffalo driven out by the settlers; he saw the Indian retreat as the pioneer advanced. His training is that of the old West, in its frontier days. And now the frontier opportunities are gone. Discontent is demanding an extension of governmental activity in its behalf. In these demands, it finds itself in touch with the depressed agricultural classes and the workingmen of the South and East. The Western problem is no longer a sectional problem; it is a social problem on a national scale. The greater West, extending from the Alleghanies to the Pacific, cannot be regarded as a unit; it requires analysis into regions and classes. But its area, its population, and its material resources would give force to its assertion that if there is a sectionalism in the country, the sectionalism is Eastern. The old West, united to the new South, would produce, not a new sectionalism, but a new Americanism. It would not mean sectional disunion, as some have speculated, but it might mean a drastic assertion of national government and imperial expansion under a popular hero.

This, then, is the real situation: a people composed of heterogeneous materials, with diverse and conflicting ideals and social interests, having passed from the task of filling up the vacant spaces of the continent, is now thrown back upon itself, and is seeking an equilibrium. The diverse elements are being fused into national unity. The forces of reorganization are turbulent and the nation seems like a witches' kettle:

> Double, double, toil and trouble,
> Fire burn and cauldron bubble.

But the far West has its centres of industrial life and culture not unlike those of the East. It has state universities, rivaling in conservative and scientific economic instruction those of any other part of the Union, and its citizens more often visit the East, than do Eastern men the West. As time goes on, its industrial development will bring it more into harmony with the East.

Moreover, the old Northwest holds the balance of power, and is the battlefield on which these issues of American development are to be settled. It has more in common with all regions of the country than has any other region. It understands the East, as the East does not understand the West. The White City which recently rose on the shores of Lake Michigan fitly typified its growing culture as well as its capacity for great achievement. Its complex and representative industrial organization and business ties, its determination to hold fast to what is original and good in its Western experience, and its readiness to learn and receive the results of the experience of other sections and nations, make it an open-minded and safe arbiter of the American destiny. In the long run the centre of the Republic may be trusted to strike a wise balance between the contending ideals. But she does not deceive herself; she knows that the problem of the West means nothing less than the problem of working out original social ideals and social adjustment for the American nation.

John D. Hicks: THE FARMERS' GRIEVANCES

With John D. Hicks Populism received its most detailed, scholarly treatment at the hands of a sympathetic historian. In this selection from his comprehensive study, The Populist Revolt: A History of the Farmer's Alliance and the People's Party (1931), *Hicks describes the economic and political grievances that underlay agrarian radicalism.*

IN THE spring of 1887 a North Carolina farm journal stated with rare accuracy what many farmers in all sections of the United States had been thinking for some time.

There is something radically wrong in our industrial system. There is a screw loose. The wheels have dropped out of balance. The railroads have never been so prosperous, and yet agriculture languishes. The banks have never done a better or more profitable business, and yet agriculture languishes. Manufacturing enterprises never made more money or were in a more flourishing condition, and yet agriculture languishes. Towns and cities flourish and "boom" and grow and "boom," and yet agriculture languishes. Salaries and fees were never so temptingly high and desirable, and yet agriculture languishes. . . .

The farmer never doubted that his lack of prosperity was directly traceable to the low prices he received for the commodities he had to sell. The period from 1870 to 1897 was one of steadily declining prices. . . .

So low did the scale of prices drop that in certain sections of the country it was easy enough to prove, statistically at least, that farming was carried on only at an actual loss. It was generally agreed that seven or eight cents of the price recevied for each pound of cotton went to cover the cost of production; by the later eighties, moreover, many cotton growers were finding it necessary to market their crops for less than they had been getting. The average price per bushel received by northwestern wheat growers dropped as low as from forty-two to forty-eight cents, whereas the cost of raising a bushel of wheat was variously estimated at from forty-five to sixty-seven cents. Statisticians held that it cost about twenty-one cents to produce a bushel of corn, but the western farmer sometimes had to take less than half that sum. . . .

Not politicians only but many other who studied the question held that overproduction was the root of the evil. Too many acres were being tilled, with the result that too many bushels of grain, too many bales of cotton, too many tons of

The Populist Revolt, a History of the Farmer's Alliance and the People's Party by John D. Hicks. pp. 54–94. The University of Minnesota Press, Minneapolis. Copyright 1931 by the University of Minnesota.

hay, too many pounds of beef were being thrown upon the market each year. As the population increased, the number of consumers had advanced correspondingly, but the increase in production had gone on even more rapidly. . . .

Those who believed in the overproduction theory argued that to some extent this condition of affairs was due to the rapid expansion of the agricultural frontier in the United States and in the world at large. In the United States the opportunity to obtain free lands, or lands at a nominal price, tempted thousands of artisans and laborers to seek their fortunes in the West. This was true not only in the Northwest, where wheat and corn were the chief products, but also in the Southwest, where the main reliance was placed in cotton. . . .

Moreover, the revolution in means of transportation that had been accomplished during the latter half of the nineteenth century had opened up world markets for regions that had hitherto had small chance to sell their produce. This was true not only of the American West, which could never have come into being without an elaborate system of railways over which to market its crops, but also of distant regions in Russia, India, Australia, Algeria, Canada, Mexico, and the Argentine, whence, thanks to railways and steamship lines, harvests of surpassing abundance could now find their way to the very centers of trade. Such crops as wheat and cotton, of which the United States had an excess for export, must now often come into competition with these tremendous outpourings from other parts of the world, and the prices must be fixed accordingly. . . .

But the farmers and their defenders refused to place much stock in the overproduction theory. Admitting that the output from the farm had increased per-

haps even more rapidly than population, they could still argue that this in itself was not sufficient to account for the low prices and the consequent agricultural depression. They pointed out that, with the general improvement of conditions among the masses, consumption had greatly increased. Possibly the demand attendant upon this fact alone would be nearly, if not quite, sufficient to offset the greater yearly output. There would be, moreover, even heavier consumption were it possible for those who needed and wanted more of the products of the farm to buy to the full extent of their ability to consume. . . . Were there not "certain influences at work, like thieves in the night," to rob the farmers of the fruits of their toil?

Many of the farmers thought that there were; and they were not always uncertain as to the identity of those who stood in the way of agricultural prosperity. Western farmers blamed many of their troubles upon the railroads, by means of which all western crops must be sent to market. There was no choice but to use these roads, and as the frontier advanced farther and farther into the West, the length of the haul to market increased correspondingly. Sometimes western wheat or corn was carried a thousand, perhaps even two thousand, miles before it could reach a suitable place for export or consumption. For these long hauls the railroads naturally exacted high rates, admittedly charging "all the traffic would bear." . . .

Local freight rates were particularly high. The railroads figured, not without reason, that large shipments cost them less per bushel to haul than small shipments. The greater the volume of traffiic the less the cost of carrying any portion of that traffic. Accordingly, on through routes and long hauls where there was a

large and dependable flow of freight
the rates were comparatively low — the
lower because for such runs there was
usually ample competition. Rates from
Chicago to New York, for example, were
low in comparison with rates for similar
distances from western points to Chicago,
while between local points west of Chicago the rates were even more dispro-
portionate. . . .

Only rarely did the shipper have a
choice of two or more railway companies with which to deal, and even
when he had this choice there was not invariably competition. The roads reached
agreements among themselves; more
than that, they consolidated. . . . Throughout the eighties as the number of miles
of railroad increased, the number of
railroad companies tended to decrease.
Communities that prided themselves
upon a new "parallel and competing
line" were apt to discover "some fine
morning that enough of its stock had
been purchased by the older lines to give
them control." Thus fortified by monopoly, the railroads, as the farmer saw it,
could collect whatever rates they chose.

* * *

It was commonly belived also that the
practice of stock-watering had much to
do with the making of high rates. The exact extent to which the railroads watered
their stock, or to which a particular railroad watered its stock, would be a difficult matter to determine, but that the
practice did exist in varying degrees
seems not to be open to question. A writer
in Poor's *Manual* for 1884 stated that the
entire four billion dollars at which the
railways of the United States were capitalized represented nothing but so much
"water." So sweeping a statement seems
rather questionable, but the belief was
general that railroad companies got their

actual funds for investment from bond
issues and passed out stocks to the share-
holders for nothing. . . .

High rates due to overcapitalization
and other causes were not, however, the
sole cause of dissatisfaction with the railways. It was commonly asserted that the
transportation companies discriminated
definitely against the small shipper and
in favor of his larger competitors. The
local grain merchant without elevator facilities or the farmer desirous of shipping
his own grain invariably had greater and
graver difficulties with the roads than did
the large elevator companies. These latter, the farmers contended, were favored
by "inside rates," by rebates, and by pref-
erential treatment with regard to cars.

* * *

The indictment against the railroads
was the stronger in view of their political
activites. It is not unfair to say that nor-
mally the railroads — sometimes a single
road — dominated the political situation
in every western state. In Kansas the
Santa Fe was all-powerful; in Nebraska
the Burlington and the Union Pacific
shared the control of the state; everywhere the political power of one or more
of the roads was a recognized fact. Railway influence was exerted in practically
every important nominating convention
to insure that no one hostile to the railways should be named for office. Railway lobbyists were on hand whenever a
legislature met to see that measures un-
favorable to the roads were quietly eliminated. Railway taxation, a particularly
tender question, was always watched
with the greatest solicitude and, from the
standpoint of the prevention of high
taxes, usually with the greatest of success. How much bribery and corruption
and intrigue the railroads used to secure
the ends they desired will never be

known. For a long time, however, by fair means or foul, their wishes in most localities were closely akin to law. Beyond a doubt whole legislatures were sometimes bought and sold.

In the purchase of men of influence railway passes were ever of the greatest potency. Members of the legislatures pocketed the mileage they were allowed by the state and rode back and forth to the capital on passes furnished by the railroads. Governors, judges, railway commissioners, and all other public officials were given passes and were encouraged to use them freely. Prominent attorneys were similarly privileged and in addition were generally retained by the railroads. The makers of public opinion — editors, ministers, and local politicians — were not neglected; when they were too insignificant to merit the regulation annual pass, they were given occasional free trips or half-fare permits. . . .

But from the standpoint of the western pioneer the crowning infamy of the railroads was their theft, as it appeared to him, of his lands. Free lands, or at least cheap lands, had been his ever since America was. Now this "priceless heritage" was gone, disposed of in no small part to the railroads. To them the national government had donated an area "larger than the territory occupied by the great German empire," land which, it was easy enough to see, should have been preserved for the future needs of the people. For this land the railroads charged the hapless emigrant from "three to ten prices" and by a pernicious credit system forced him into a condition of well-nigh perpetual "bondage." "Only a little while ago," ran one complaint, "the people owned this princely domain. Now they are *starving for land* — starving for an opportunity to labor — starving for the right to create from the soil a subsis-

tence for their wives and little children." To the western farmers of this generation the importance of the disappearance of free lands was not a hidden secret to be unlocked only by the researches of some future historian. It was an acutely oppressive reality. . . .

Complaints against the railways, while most violent in the West, were by no means confined to that section. Practically every charge made by the western farmers had its counterpart elsewhere. In the South particularly the sins that the roads were held to have committed differed in degree, perhaps, but not much in kind, from the sins of the western roads. . . .

In the northwestern grain-growing states the problem of the railroads was closely related to the problem of the elevators. Some grain houses were owned by individuals or local companies who ran one or more elevators in neighboring towns. A few were owned by the railway companies themselves. Still others were the property of large corporations that operated a whole string of elevators up and down the entire length of a railway line. These large companies naturally built better and more commodious houses than the smaller ones; they were more efficient in their manner of doing business; and they were easily the favorites of the railroads. All the companies, large or small, must obtain on whatever terms the railway companies saw fit to impose such special privileges as the right to build upon railroad land and the right to proper sidetrack facilities. By refusing these favors the roads could prevent, and did prevent, the erection of new elevators where they deemed the old ones adequate, but once an elevator was authorzied it could usually count on railway support.

Thanks mainly to their satisfactory relations with the railroads, the first elevator companies to cover a territory enjoyed in their respective localities almost a complete monopoly of the grain business, both buying and selling. Wherever elevators existed the roads virtually requried that shipments of grain be made through them, for in practice if not in theory cars were seldom furnished to those who wished to avoid the elevator and to load their grain from wagons or from flat warehouses. On the face of it this rule seemed harmless enough, for the elevator companies were supposedly under obligations to serve the general public and to ship grain from all comers on equal terms. This they might have done with fair impartiality had they not been engaged themselves in the buying and selling of grain. But since it was the chief concern of the elevator operator to purchase and ship all the grain he could get, he could hardly be expected to take much interest in providing facilities for the farmer who wished to ship directly or for the competitive grain merchant who lacked an elevator of his own. The result was that the independent buyer was speedily "frozen out," and the farmer found that if he was to get rid of his grain at all he must sell to the local elevator for whatever price he was offered. He claimed rightly that under such a system he was denied a free market for his grain. To all except the privileged elevator companies the market was closed.

* * *

If the farmer had little part in fixing the price at which his produce sold, he had no part at all in fixing the price of the commodities for which his earnings were spent. Neither did competition among manufacturers and dealers do much in the way of price-fixing, for the

age of "big business," of trusts, combines, pools, and monopolies, had come. These trusts, as the farmers saw it, joined with the railroads, and if necessary with the politicians, "to hold the people's hands and pick their pockets." They "bought raw material at their own price, sold the finished product at any figure they wished to ask, and rewarded labor as they saw fit." Through their machinations "the farmer and the workingman generally" were "overtaxed right and left." . . .

The protective tariff, while not universally deplored in farm circles, met with frequent criticism as a means of "protecting one class at the expense of another — the manufacturer against the farmer, the rich against the poor." Because of the tariff the American market was reserved for the exclusive exploitation of the American manufacturer, whose prices were fixed not in accordance with the cost of production but in accordance with the amount of protection he was able to secure. The genial system of logrolling, which on occasion made Democrats as good protectionists as Republicans, insured a high degree of protection all around. And so the tariff became a veritable "hot-bed for the breeding of trusts and combines among all classes of men thus sheltered by the law." This situation was the more intolerable from the farmer's point of view for the reason that he must sell at prices fixed by foreign competition. The protective tariff gave the eastern manufacturer "the home market at protective prices," but the prices of western and southern farm produce were "fixed by the surplus sold in foreign free-trade markets." . . .

It was the grinding burden of debt, however, that aroused the farmers, both southern and western, to action. The widespread dependence upon crop liens in the South and farm mortgages in the

West has already been described. In the
South as long as the price of cotton continued high and in the West as long as
the flow of eastern capital remained un-
interrepted, the grievances against the
railroads, the middlemen, and the tariff-
protected trusts merely smouldered. But
when the bottom dropped out of the
cotton market and the western boom
collapsed, then the weight of debt was
keenly felt and frenzied agitation began.
The eastern capitalists were somehow to
blame. They had conspired together to
defraud the farmers — "to levy tribute
upon the productive energies of West
and South.". . .

As one hard season succeeded another
the empty-handed farmer found his back
debts and unpaid interest becoming an
intolerable burden. In the West after the
crisis of 1887 interest rates, already high,
rose still higher. Farmers who needed
money to renew their loans, to meet par-
tial payments on their land, or to tide
them over to another season were told,
truly enough, that money was very
scarce. The flow of eastern capital to the
West had virtually ceased. The various
mortgage companies that had been doing
such a thriving business a few months
before had now either gone bankrupt or
had made drastic retrenchments. Rates
of seven or eight per cent on real estate
were not regarded as extremely low; and
on chattels ten or twelve per cent was
considered very liberal, from eighteen to
twenty-four per cent was not uncommon,
and forty per cent or above was not un-
known. Naturally the number of real
estate mortgages placed dropped off pre-
cipitately. Instead of the six thousand,
worth nearly $5,500,000, that had been
placed in Nebraska during the years 1884
to 1887, there were in the three years following 1887 only five hundred such mortgages, worth only about $650,000, while

only one out of four of the farm mortgages held on South Dakota land in 1892
had been contracted prior to 1887. When
the farmer could no longer obtain money
on his real estate, he usually mortgaged
his chattels, with the result that in many
localities nearly everything that could
carry a mortgage was required to do so.
In Nebraska during the early nineties the
number of these badges of "dependence
and slavery" recorded by the state audi-
tor averaged over half a million annually.
In Dakota many families were kept from
leaving for the East only by the fact that
their horses and wagons were mortgaged and could therefore not be taken
beyond the state boundaries. . . .

Usually the mortgagor was highly protected by the terms of the mortgage and
could foreclose whenever an interest pay-
ment was defaulted, whether the principal was due or not. In the late eighties
and the early nineties foreclosures came
thick and fast. Kansas doubtless suffered
most on this account, for from 1889 to
1893 over eleven thousand farm mortgages were foreclosed in this state, and
in some counties as much as ninety per
cent of the farm lands passed into the
ownership of the loan companies. It was
estimated by one alarmist that "land
equal to a tract thirty miles wide and
ninety miles long had been foreclosed
and bought in by the loan companies of
Kansas in a year." Available statistics
would seem to bear out this assertion,
but the unreliability of such figures is notorious. Many farmers and speculators,
some of them perfectly solvent, deliberately invited foreclosure because they
found after the slump that their land was
mortgaged for more than it was worth.
On the other hand, many cases of genuine bankruptcy were settled out of court
and without record. But whatever the
unreliability of statistics the fact remains

that in Kansas and neighboring states the number of farmers who lost their lands because of the hard times and crop failures was very large.

In the South the crop-lien system constituted the chief mortgage evil and the chief grievance, but a considerable amount of real and personal property was also pledged for debt. Census statistics, here also somewhat unreliable because of the numerous informal and unrecorded agreements, show that in Georgia about one-fifth of the taxable acres were under mortgage, and a special investigation for the same state seemed to prove that a high proportion of the mortgage debt was incurred to meet current expenditures rather than to acquire more land or to make permanent improvements. Similar conditions existed throughout the cotton South. Chattel mortgages were also freely given, especially by tenants, but frequently also by small proprietors. Interests rates were as impossibly high as in the West, and foreclosures almost as inevitable. . . . .

Taxation added a heavy burden to the load of the farmer. Others might conceal their property. The merchant might underestimate the value of his stock, the householder might neglect to list a substantial part of his personal property, the holder of taxable securities might keep his ownership a secret, but the farmer could not hide his land. If it was perhaps an exaggeration to declare that the farmers "represent but one-fourth of the nation's wealth and they pay three-fourths of the taxes," it was probably true enough that land bore the chief brunt of taxation, both in the South and in the West. . . .

Beset on every hand by demands for funds — funds with which to meet his obligations to the bankers, the loan companies, or the tax collectors and funds with which to maintain his credit with the merchants so that he might not lack the all-essential seed to plant another crop or the few necessities of life that he and his family could not contrive either to produce for themselves or to go without — the farmer naturally enough raised the battle cry of "more money." He came to believe that, after all, his chief grievance was against the system of money and banking, which now virtually denied him credit and which in the past had only plunged him deeper and deeper into debt. There must be something more fundamentally wrong than the misdeeds of railroads and trusts and tax assessors. Why should dollars grow dearer and dearer and scarcer and scarcer? Why, indeed, unless because of the manipulations of those to whom such a condition would bring a profit?

Much agitation by greenbackers and by free-silverites and much experience in the marketing of crops had made clear even to the most obtuse, at least of the debtors, that the value of a dollar was greater than it once had been. It would buy two bushels of grain where formerly it would buy only one. It would buy twelve pounds of cotton where formerly it would buy but six. The orthodox retort of the creditor to such a statement was that too much grain and cotton were being produced — the overproduction theory. But, replied the debtor, was this the whole truth? Did not the amount of money in circulation have something to do with the situation? Currency reformers were wont to point out that at the close of the Civil War the United States had nearly two billions of dollars in circulation. Now the population had doubled and the volume of business had probably trebled, but the number of dollars in circulation had actually declined! Was not each dollar overworked? Had it not attained on this account a fictitious value?

Whatever the explanation, it was clear enough that the dollar, expressed in any other terms than itself, had appreciated steadily in value ever since the Civil War. The depreciated greenback currency, in which all ordinary business was transacted until 1879, reached by that year a full parity with gold. But the purchasing power of the dollar still continued its upward course. For this phenomenon the quantity theory may be — probably is — an insufficient explanation, but . . . the fact of continuous appreciation can hardly be denied.

For those farmers who were free from debt and were neither investors nor borrowers such a condition might have had little meaning. The greater purchasing power of the dollar meant fewer dollars for their crops, but it meant also fewer dollars spent for labor and supplies. Conceivably, the same degree of prosperity could be maintained on the smaller income. But in the West and in the South the number of debt-free farmers was small indeed, and for the debtor the rising value of the dollar was a serious matter. The man who gave a long-term mortgage on his real estate was in the best position to appreciate how serious it was. Did he borrow a thousand dollars on his land for a five-year term, then he must pay back at the end of the allotted time a thousand dollars. But it might well be that, whereas at the time he had contracted the loan a thousand dollars meant a thousand bushels of wheat or ten thousand pounds of cotton, at the time he must pay it the thousand dollars meant fifteen hundred bushels of wheat or fifteen thousand pounds of cotton. . . .

Add to this the unreasonably high interest rates usually exacted and the commissions and deductions that were rarely omitted, and the plight of the debtor farmer becomes painfully clear. He was paying what would have amounted to about a twenty or twenty-five per cent rate of interest on a non-appreciating dollar.

It was, moreover, far from comforting to reflect that in such a transaction what was one man's loss was another's gain. Nor was it surprising that the harassed debtor imputed to the creditor, to whose advantage the system worked, a deliberate attempt to cause the dollar to soar to ever greater and greater heights. Had not the creditor class ranged itself solidly behind the Resumption Act of 1875, by which the greenback dollar had been brought to a parity with gold? Was not the same class responsible for the "crime of 1873," which had demonetized silver and by just so much had detracted from the quantity of the circulating medium? Was there not, indeed, a nefarious conspiracy of creditors — eastern creditors, perhaps with English allies — to increase their profits at the expense of the debtors — western and southern — by a studied manipulation of the value of the dollar? . . .

Nor was this grievance confined to resentment against the steadily mounting value of the dollar. There was in addition an undeniable and apparently unreaonable fluctuation in its purchasing power during any given year. . . .

Southerners and westerners who studied the question found an answer in the inelasticity of the currency. In agricultural sections, they reasoned, money was needed most when crops were harvested, for at such times the fruit of an entire year's productive effort was thrown upon the market. The farmer could not hold his crop, for he must have money with which to meet pressing obligations — store debts, interest charges, mortgages.

Sell he must, and sell he did. But this tremendous demand upon the currency increased the value of the dollar, since there were no more dollars in circulation at crop-moving time than at any other time! When at last the crop was moved and the abnormal demand for money had subsided, then the value of the dollar declined and prices rose correspondingly. These fluctuations within a given year were often large enough to make the difference between prosperity and adversity for the farmer. Could he have sold at the maximum price, or even at the average price, instead of at the minimum, he would have had far less of which to complain. As it was, he could see no good reason why the supply of money should remain constant when the need for it was variable. Unless, perchance, this were the deliberate intent of those who stood to profit from the situation. . . .

This inelasticity of the currency, as well as its inadequacy, was blamed in large part upon the national banking system, against which every critic of the monetary situation railed. According to these critics the laws establishing national banks were "of the same character of vicious legislation that demonetized silver." They were "conceived in infamy and . . . for no other purpose but to rob the many for the benefit of the few." It was at least susceptible of demonstration that the national bank-note circulation had steadily dwindled. The law of 1864 provided that national bankers must buy bonds of the United States to the extent of not less than one-third of their capital stock. These bonds were then deposited with the government and upon them as security the banks might issue notes up to ninety per cent of the par value of the bonds. This right to issue paper money, however, was exercised more freely in the years directly following the Civil War

than later on, and in 1873 the total bank-note circulation had mounted to $339,-000,000. From that time on it tended to decline. In 1876 it was $291,000,000; in 1891 it was only $168,000,000. . . .

The explanation of this cut in the note issues of national banks is not hard to find. The national debt was being paid off and some of the bonds upon which note issues had been based were retired on this account. Indeed, with its yearly revenues far in excess of its necessary expenditures, the government relaxed the rule with regard to the minimum bond deposit required of the banks and even entered the market to buy back national bonds before they were due. Naturally the bonds rose to a heavy premium, and national bankers found that they could make a greater profit by selling their bonds and retiring their notes than by keeping their notes in circulation. But in the whole proceeding the western and southern debtors saw something sinister. Was not the government in league with the money sharks to increase the value of the dollar? Why should the government bonds be paid off in gold, or its equivalent, rather than in new issues of greenbacks, the kind of money that had been used ordinarily in the purchase of these bonds? Why should there be any national banks at all? Why should "the business of issuing money and controlling its volume" be turned over "to a few persons who used their power to their own interest?" Why should not the government itself issue money direct to the people and at reasonable rates?

The argument for government issues of greenbacks had at least one dependable leg to stand upon. Such a policy would promote flexibility in the currency. The volume of note issues might then be regulated in accordance with the demand, whereas under the national banking system the volume was regulated chiefly by the possible profit to the bankers concerned. If it paid the banks to buy bonds and turn them into currency, then the banks could be expected to follow that course. If it paid better, however, to keep their bond holdings static or even to dispose of bonds and retire notes, then they followed that course. Not the needs of the country but the probable profits of the bankers de-termined the amount of the currency. The charge was made that at certain critical times, especially during crop-moving seasons, scarcity of money was deliberately connived at, since higher rates of interest could then be charged, presumably with greater profits. Probably this charge was baseless in the main, but that the currency was virtually inflexible under the national banking system is a matter of common knowledge.

Chester McArthur Destler: THE SOURCES OF WESTERN RADICALISM

Chestler McArthur Destler is the author of numerous studies of American reform and reformers, including a biography of Henry Demarest Lloyd. Although his approach to Populism does not fundamentally differ from Hicks's, Destler emphasizes the urban origin of many important ideas usually identified with the agrarian revolt.

ALTHOUGH students of western history have long contended for the existence of a unique agrarianism in the region after 1865, they . . . have failed to establish the existence there of a distinctive school of radical thought. Insulated by the continued influence of the frontier hypothesis from the records of contemporary or preceding urban movements within or without the region, and preoccupied largely with local sources of information, they have based the traditional story of western radicalism upon the assumption of an isolated, rural development undisturbed by external influences other than those affecting the marketing of farm surpluses. The singularly barren result, so far as knowledge of fundamental tenets or their implications is concerned, must be attributed to the conviction that radicalism in the American West was exclusively the product of repetitive sociological and economic processes at work on the frontier, which found expression in a somewhat emotional discontent or in a patchwork of remedial proposals that lacked any philosophical basis other than a desire to restore the working propriety of a small entrepreneur, rural economy. An escape from this *cul de sac* has been suggested by the new emphasis upon the region's participation in the technological, urban, and intellectual movements of the late nineteenth century that was urged upon historians nearly a decade ago. The late Marcus L. Hansen stressed particularly the need for study of the processes of cultural importation and acclimatization that were intensified in the West by the

From Chester McArthur Destler, "Western Radicalism, 1865–1901: Concepts and Origins," *Mississippi Valley Historical Review*, Vol. XXXI (December 1944), pp. 335–68. Reprinted by permission of The Organization of American Historians.

quickened communication and huge population movements of the period. . . .

The existence in the Upper Mississippi Valley, in 1865, of a system of democratic thought derived from an earlier integration of urban radicalism with the coonskin democracy of the hardwood frontier, suggests that subsequent intercourse between urban and agrarian radicals occurred within a conceptual pattern common to both. William Trimble has shown how the working-class Locofocoism of the Jacksonian era was transplanted by the westward movement to the rich soil of the Middle West in the forties and fifties. There it fused with the similar but less well-defined conceptions of the Benton Democracy in neighboring upland southern areas of settlement. It was reproduced so completely by wheat farmers on the prairies and oak openings farther to the north that insistence upon "equal rights" and intense hostility to monopoly, chartered corporations, banks, and the "money power" are to this day frequently regarded as peculiar to the rural mind. . . .

The revival of the democratic movement in the trans-Allegheny states after the Civil War was more than the resurgence of ante-bellum quarrels provoked by exclusively western impulses. It offers the first clear illustrations in this period of the effect of intercourse and co-operation between eastern and western, urban-born and agrarian movements upon the development of western radical thought and action. This is notably true of the antimonopoly sentiment that flourished in the western states in the half dozen years before the panic of 1873. Although rural grievances against a railroad and steamboat combination in the Upper Mississippi Valley furnished the initial impetus, and the Locofoco heritage supplied the intellectual foundation, the continuing antimonopoly movement of these years cannot be fully understood without reference to mercantile interests, the National Labor Union, and the activities of several propaganda organizations that operated from central offices on the eastern seaboard. Resentment against the extortions and monopolistic practices of the railroads was not peculiar to western farmers. It was shared by western merchants, eastern importers and shippers, the producers and refiners of the Pennsylvania oil region, and laboring men as well. It is not surprising to find in 1867 a National Anti-Monopoly Cheap Freight Railway League with headquarters in New York City. Although not much is known of this interesting organization, the private papers of its secretary reveal a far-flung agitation in behalf of cheaper railroad and telegraph rates that was directed from the eastern metropolis. . . .

The propaganda stimulus to the western antimonopoly movement was even more noteworthy in the case of the American Free-Trade League, whose headquarters were also in New York City. It was financed there largely by New York importers and by manufacturers' and shipping agents dealing with Great Britain, who had an immediate interest in the reduction of the war tariff. Although its technique bore a striking resemblance to that of the Anti-Corn Law movement, the leaders of the Free-Trade League were avowedly disciples of "the peculiar Free Trade doctrines of William Leggett," the prophet of Locofocoism. Chief of these was William Cullen Bryant, editor of the New York *Evening Post* and persistent champion of the Locofoco creed, who was president of the League during its formative years. By 1869 the free traders had expanded their activities into an intensive, far-flung propaganda campaign among the wage earners of the seaboard and westward in the interior towns and farming districts of Ohio, Illinois, Missouri, Iowa, Wisconsin, Minnesota, and California. Its numerous tracts, circulated by over half a million annually by *colporteurs* and voluntary workers, the numerous public meetings stimulated in all the important towns of the West, and tariff reform copy supplied gratis to an extensive list of western newspapers that were supported by paid advertisements, were reenforced by branch leagues in Cincinnati, Chicago, St. Louis, and San Francisco, which were financed in part by eastern funds. . . .

The synchronism of the propaganda of the Cheap Freight Railway League and the Free-Trade League with the continuing antimonopoly movement in the West, is in itself highly suggestive. It is obvious that the revival of Locofoco stereotypes in the Mississippi Valley was but part of a nation-wide development that was shared by all the elements that suffered from the high tariff and the abuses of railroad and telegraph management. . . .

Most students of western radicalism had overlooked the dual character of the Greenback agitation that spread so rapidly after the panic of 1873. Judged by its origins Greenbackism was at once a western inflationist proposal and an eastern radical philosophy by means of which its urban working-class adherents sought to substitute a co-operative economy for the mercantile and industrial capitalism of the day. . . .

[This second phase], for want of a more distinguishing name, must be termed Kelloggism. Its author, Edward Kellogg, had been a New York merchant during the Locofoco period. Forced into assignment by the panic of 1837, he had found in the usurious manipulation of currency and credit by privately owned banks the cause of periodic depressions and of the concentration of wealth. Arguing that monetary policy and banking were strictly governmental functions, he sought to supplant private and state banks with a national banking and currency system to be operated exclusively by the central government. Its outstanding features were to be a flexible currency, loans on real estate at low rates, and interchangeability of the paper currency with government bonds. Such a system with its low interest rates, Kellogg taught, would destroy money monopoly, secure to labor its just reward, lower rents, and promote the development of rural society. His book, *Labor and Other Capital*, was republished in successive editions after 1860 and became a classic of American radicalism, the "Bible" of currency reformers until shunted aside by the free-silver craze of the nineties. . . .

Space is lacking to trace in detail the interaction of the two currency agitations upon each other and of both upon the agricultural West through the next three decades. . . .

Eventually the National Farmers' Alliance, led by Jay Burrows, a disciple of Kellogg's, embodied the land loan plan in its platform while the southern Alliance advanced from this to the noted "subtreasury" scheme as an adaptation more attractive to staple farming. Government loans of greenbacks to farmers on land or crop mortgage security became the central feature in the platforms of farm organizations from 1886–1892, of the Union Labor Party in 1888, and of the Populists in 1892. . . .

The co-operative movement is another example of the readiness with which western agrarians borrowed urban formulas ready-made in their attempts to solve agricultural problems. In this case European experience was clearly drawn upon, while the influence of organized labor in America upon the farming co-operative movements seems also indubitable. Although ante-bellum *Arbeiterbund* experiments and agitation by Horace Greeley may have suggested the feasibility of a co-operative movement, the first vigorous development of productive and distributive co-operation in the United States occurred after Appomattox in the urban centers of the East and the Ohio Valley. There workmen in all leading trades experimented with co-operative workshops and patronized co-operative stores. This movement was vigorously espoused by William L. Sylvis and the National Labor Union as "a sure and lasting remedy for the abuses of the present industrial system." . . . Western antimonopolists, whose delegates attended the congresses of the National Labor Union, learned there of the co-operative plans of the wage earners. . . . Eventually the Grangers adopted the Rochdale plan of consumers' co-operation and made direct contact with the English Co-operative Union. The revival of interest in co-operation among western and southern farmers during the eighties followed hard upon the renewed agitation of the idea by the Knights of Labor who were the greatest agency then propagating knowledge of European and American co-operative experiments in the United States. Its contact with the farmers increased rather than diminished after its catastrophic defeats in 1886 since it deliberately penetrated the country towns and rural areas of the East in search of recruits. Thus, while the ideological impulse to the co-operative experiments of the Farmers' Alliance movement was partially derived from surviving Granger experiments or drawn directly from British experience, a portion at least came from the American labor

movement. In this period, also, co-operative creameries were introduced into the Middle West from Scandinavia by Danish immigrants. . . .

Western cities made significant contributions to the radical movements of the rural West and urban East in the seventies and eighties. The wider antimonopoly movement that was directed against industrial combinations and speculative manipulation of commodity prices received its initial impetus from Henry Demarest Lloyd. His antimonopolism was derived from a Locofoco family background. It was confirmed by four years' work as assistant secretary of the American Free-Trade League. After this he joined the staff of the Chicago *Tribune*. First as its financial editor and then as its chief editorial writer, he campaigned for over a decade for reform of the Chicago Board of Trade, exposed the looting of western mining companies by rings of insiders, described the daily misdeeds and monopolistic practices of the railroads, and attacked the Standard Oil Company and other trusts as they emerged into public view. He lent vigorous support, also, to the agrarian demand that Congress establish a strong, national rate-fixing commission in control of the railroads and a postal telegraph to be operated by the national government in competition with the Western Union. He then turned to a wider public in a series of impressive magazine articles that laid bare the implications of the combination movement for democracy in America and demanded its control through further extension of the regulatory powers of the state. These articles with his editorials and other contributions in the *Tribune* initiated the antitrust movement that was superimposed upon the continuing struggle with the railroads in the West. Diverted from journalism to a career of social reform, Lloyd continued the fight against monopoly by publication of his great work, *Wealth against Commonwealth*, and by participation in the Populist revolt. Until after its collapse he was regarded by the western agrarians as one of their chief inspirers.

An equally notable contribution to American radicalism came from San Francisco and Oakland, California, urban centers developing within a few hundred miles of the mining and agricultural frontier of the Far West. There Henry George, another journalist, but onetime Philadelphia printer's devil, perfected the single-tax theory in the midst of a prolonged struggle with the West Coast monopolies. An admirer of Jefferson, a Jacksonian Democrat of the Locofoco tradition, he saw in land monopoly the cause of poverty. By taxing away the unearned increment in land values, or virtually confiscating ground rents, he would break up the great speculative holdings in the West, check the dissipation of the national domain, and weaken franchise monopolies of all kinds. Abolition of all other taxes would destroy the monopolies dependent upon the protective tariff. Thus a single, decisive use of the taxing power would restore both liberty and equality of opportunity to American economic life while at the same time it would check the urban movement, revive agriculture, and enrich rural life. After leading a fruitless land reform movement on the West Coast during the depressed seventies, Henry George moved to New York City where he published *Progress and Poverty* in 1880. Its appeal to natural rights, its indictment of the existing business system, its moral overtones and moving appeal to the traditions of humanitarian democracy, and its utopian panacea all exerted a profound influence upon public opinion in

Ireland, Great Britain, and the United States. In a crusade for social justice that continued until his dramatic death in 1897, George exercised an unprecedented influence upon the American labor movement. He awakened journalists, intellectuals, small capitalists, and young lawyers to a comprehension of the grave economic and social problems of the rising urban world. His system of democratic economics dealt the first shattering blow to the economic determinism derived from the "Manchester School" and to the Social Darwinism that discouraged all attempts to remedy social evils or shackle the anarchic business of the day. Independent labor politics, municipal reform, and the development of a more public-spirited political leadership received direct and powerful impetus from the single-tax movement in eastern and midwestern cities between 1880 and 1900, while the single-tax panacea offered to discontented workers, farmers, small capitalists, and intellectuals an alternative to Marxian Socialism that promised social justice while preserving the old individualism. Most leaders of the Farmers' Alliance movement refused to accept the single tax as "the universal solvent that will melt away the social and industrial ills that afflict our nation." The agitation for the single tax, nevertheless, did much to increase agrarian interest in the land question, while "Sockless Jerry" Simpson, Populist Congressman from Kansas in the nineties, was an earnest disciple of Henry George. In this decade, also, the support given by George A. Schilling and the powerful single-tax bloc in the Illinois Federation of Labor was an important factor in the election and progressive administration of John P. Altgeld. Although the exact extent of Henry George's influence upon the rural West remains to be determined, the sin-

gle-tax movement is an outstanding illus-
tration of the far-flung influence of a
western but urban-born school of thought
upon proletarian movements and middle-
class liberalism in regions as far distant
as the Atlantic seaboard, the British Isles,
and Australasia.

During the late eighties an urban, eastern, American-born socialist movement
attracted interest in the cities and farming areas of the West. Known as Nationalism it developed spontaneously from
enthusiasm provoked by Edward Bellamy's *Looking Backward*. Converts to
Bellamy's utopia of a highly centralized,
almost militarized socialist commonwealth organized Nationalist Clubs as far
west as California. Members and officials
of the Farmers' Alliance, trades unions,
the Knights of Labor, and a few outstanding railroad executives joined the
movement. The earlier antimonopoly
movements and the propaganda of the
Knights of Labor had prepared the soil
well for sowing Nationalist principles
among western agrarians. It is not surprising, therefore, to find N. B. Ashby,
lecturer of the National Farmers' Alliance, endorsing Nationalism "as the
only true and effectual cure" for "the
social question," and as the logical, evo-
lutionary fulfillment of the nation's destiny. With Nationalist clubs active in
fourteen Middle and Far Western states
the organizers of the People's Party were
almost compelled to invite them to send
delegates to the Cincinnati Conference
of May, 1891, where five Nationalists
helped to frame the first national manifesto of the Populist revolt. At the subsequent conventions at St. Louis and
Omaha in 1892, the Nationalists joined
with the Knights in giving effective support to the "transportation plank" in the
revised platform. So gratified were they
at its adoption that the Nationalists gave

Populism such wholehearted support
that Nationalism lost its identity in the
People's Party. To its strength Bellamy's
followers contributed especially in the
eastern states, although he continued to
enjoy considerable influence with the
older antimonopoly element in the
West. . . .

This analysis suggests that in Populism
may be found the system of radical
thought that emerged in the West from
three decades of recurring unrest, agitation, and intercourse with radical and
reform movements in the urban world.
Although scholars have studied it as a
political movement or as the product of
social and economic conditions, as a
school of thought Populism has been
rarely, if ever, subjected to the careful
analysis that Socialism, Anarchism, or
Communism have received. Yet the
Populists themselves regarded Populism
as a faith and a creed as well as a program. They exhibited, furthermore, a
clear sense of continuity with preceding
radical movements. . . .

At first glance the program that
emerged from this process seemed like a
"crazy-quilt" of unrelated and "crackpot"
proposals. Yet it produced a fairly dur-
able synthesis, judging from the tenacity
with which the Populists reiterated their
Omaha platform on all and sundry occasions, until an era of unemployment,
mortgage foreclosures, Coxey's armies,
and industrial conflict had so heightened
the emotional overtones of the movement
that the least well-ballasted agrarians
and the professional politicians in control
of the party machinery sought quick
relief and easy victory through free
silver. It was this synthesis, under the
name of Populism, which received such
intense loyalty from its adherents and
provoked an emotional opposition from
conservative elements. Proclaimed in the

Omaha platform as the official version of the Populist creed, it must now be analyzed in an attempt to identify the basic concepts that it shared with its progenitors and to determine the extent to which it presented a well-defined system of radical thought.

Antimonopolism was the basic element in Populism. The preamble and planks of the Omaha platform of 1892 demonstrate this beyond question. The preamble denounced the corruption of democratic government by privileged business, the abuses by which a buccaneering capitalism exploited the people and created a new class of millionaires. Rather than the "sham battle over the tariff," the real issue, it declared, lay "in the formation of combines and rings," in the power of "capitalists, corporations, and national banks," "the oppressions of the usurers." The dominant antimonopoly bias of Populism was even more clearly expressed in the platform itself. This was devoted entirely to the three great fields of monopoly that had been the butt of agrarian agitation for decades: money and banking, railroads and communication, and land. The remedies proposed show clearly how far the Populists were committed to government intervention in business and to limited experiments with state socialism as a means of combating the great movement toward monopoly and economic concentration then under way in the business world. To destroy "the money power" and to solve the "financial question," to use terms employed by the presidential nominee of the party, the platform proposed an exclusively governmental currency and a combination of government operated postal savings banks and "subtreasuries." The latter "or a better system" was to loan money to farmers on crops or land at no more than two per cent interest, while

the volume of the currency was to fluctuate with the demand for agricultural credits. Irrespective of the obvious indebtedness of this financial program to the earlier agitation of Kelloggism, it is plain that money monopoly was the evil for which such a drastic extension of government activity into banking was proposed. Monopoly on the railroads and in communications was dealt with in the same manner. Here again government ownership and operation was the remedy, a solution derived from the Knights of Labor and Nationalism. Land monopoly, the third great problem dealt with, was to be remedied by government action also, in this case by restoration to the national domain of alien holdings and land held by railroads and other corporations in excess of their actual needs. The graduated income tax was proposed by the Omaha convention as the proper means of dealing with the giant fortunes accumulated through government favoritism to capitalists and usurers.

* * *

Populism's kinship with preceding radical movements in the rural and urban West and East was indicated, also, by the sympathy which its adherents gave to the co-operative idea. Now and then, as in Illinois, the State Purchasing Agent of the Farmers' Alliance was active in organizing the new party, while the Nationalists in its ranks were eager to hasten the coming of a co-operative utopia. Despite the havoc wrought by the depression upon the underfinanced co-operative organizations of the farmers, and perhaps because of the widespread distress, interest in co-operation continued among the Populists and their sympathizers. Utopian novels such as *Altruria* by William Dean Howells and *Equality* by Edward Bellamy were expressions in literature of an attitude in Populist ranks that led to the projection or establishment of a series of co-operative communities. Such was Mrs. Annie L. Diggs' proposed "Colorado Co-operative Colony," the Ruskin Co-operative Colony in Tennessee, whose *Coming Nation* had such a wide circulation in Populist ranks, or the Christian Co-operative Colony established in Georgia after the collapse of the People's Party by the former editor of the *Wealth Makers* of Lincoln, Nebraska. The American Co-operative Union was the product, in 1896, of a Congress convened at St. Louis by the co-operative elements within the People's Party simultaneously with its last great national convention. The shattered remnants of the American Railway Union, which for two years had supported Populism, organized the Brotherhood of the Co-operative Commonwealth, a few months later, by means of which they planned to colonize a western state so thoroughly with co-operative communities that they could control it politically and use the power of the state to aid them in establishing a "co-operative commonwealth." These same elements in the St. Louis convention of 1896 were part of the "middle-of-the-road" faction that remained loyal to the antimonopolism and economic collectivism of the Omaha platform. Thus in supporting the co-operative movement, whether of producers or of consumers or in especially organized communities, the Populists were seeking through private, voluntary organization in the economic field to diminish "the power of the industrial empire." This might well have been accomplished by means of "a great co-operative movement in America" as much as by government ownership of monopolies. . . .

That the Populists regarded tariff reform as a mere palliative is indicative of their determination to embark upon a revolutionary use of governmental power in subjecting the corporate business system to democratic controls. Although the free trade agitation had been an important factor in the revival of antimonopolism in the West from 1867-1872, the eastern free traders from the outset had advocated specie payments and laissez faire. Such outstanding tariff reformers of the eighties and nineties as Carl Schurz, David A. Wells, E. L. Godkin, and Grover Cleveland adhered to this position. In basic interests and sympathy they were far closer to the national banks and the existing business system than they were to the western agrarians and the Knights of Labor. In 1896 the tariff reformers were found along with William McKinley and Marcus A. Hanna on the side of the railroads, the protected industries, and high finance. Men of such stamp had little to offer to western radicals who were bent upon a drastic reorganization of American economic life through collective action by the democratic state. . . .

If Populism as a radical system was primarily economic in character, was any concept other than antimonopolism and the desirability of a semicollectivist economy fundamental to its economic theory? Careful study of the St. Louis and Omaha platforms of 1892 indicates that there was. Closely linked with declarations in favor of an alliance with urban labor is found the statement, identical in both documents: "Wealth belongs to him who creates it. Every dollar taken from industry without an equivalent is robbery. If any one will not work, neither shall he eat." This statement furnishes the second key to Populist economic thought. Its origins can be found in the early antimonopoly and Granger movements. The *Prairie Farmer's* famous cartoon of the early seventies, showing the farmer, who pays for all, surrounded by a clergyman, merchant, lawyer, legislator, soldier, railroad magnate, and doctor, expressed this theory of wealth. It had been shared by the National Labor Union, the Industrial Congress, and the Knights of Labor. More remotely, the same view had been postulated by Edward Kellogg as fundamental to his new monetary system. It was basic to the ante-bellum labor movements.

This third fundamental concept in Populist economic theory, which it inherited from earlier labor and agrarian movements, was none other than the "labor-cost theory of value" as the economists term it. Although it was derived ultimately from classical economics, it had been widely accepted in Europe and America by radicals opposed to the machine age in the sixties. In it the European anarchists and American labor reformers and agrarian leaders had found justification for their struggle against merchant capitalists and the great corporations. The labor-cost theory was derived from the conceptions of a pre-industrial age. By its application small producers, whether wheat growers and cotton farmers, or skilled laborers and small shopkeepers, sought to regain or bulwark an economic position that was being undermined by the factory age, the middleman, and monopoly capitalism. The adherents of this theory regarded capital as the product of labor alone, possessing "no independent power of production" of its own. As such, they thought that it deserved little or no reward. The whole value of the product should go to the producer, although a nominal interest might be allowed to the possessors of idle funds who loaned them to productive workers. Consumers' and producers' co-operation, the independent regulatory

commissions, a government operated banking and monetary system, government owned railroads, telegraphs, and telephones had been regarded by labor reformers and agrarian leaders as the means, not only of combating monopoly, but also of establishing an economic system in harmony with the labor-cost theory. Loyal to this philosophy of wealth the Populists at Omaha asserted that the middleman, the financier, the railroad promoters with their watered stock and monopoly rates, the bankers and mortgage holders, and the organizers of "trusts and cobines" were all nonproducers. They were profiting from bad laws and the perversion of democratic government at the expense of the producing masses who, by this process, were being so impoverished that they were "degenerating into European conditions."

Since urban labor suffered from these evils as much as the farmers, since it was denied the right to organize and, in addition, was assailed by hired bands of Pinkerton detectives, the Omaha convention urged it to join the agrarians in an independent political alliance. By means of the ballot box, they could promote a peaceful revolution in American government and economic life. "[T]he union of the labor forces of the United States this day accomplished shall be permanent and perpetual; . . . The interests of rural and civic labor are the same; their enemies are identical." Antimonopolism and the labor-cost theory of value, twin foundations in the economic theory of Populism, were thus offered to urban labor as the ideological basis of an independent farmer-laborer alliance in politics.

The desirability and practicability of such a coalition had long been an article of faith for both labor reformers and leading agrarians. Their adherence to both concepts explains the persistence with which its consummation had been sought over three decades. Attention has already been directed to repeated instances of co-operation between them. At least two attempts had been made to organize such a political party before the Populist period. . . .

The effectiveness of the Populist appeal to urban labor depended on the degree to which the labor movement still adhered to the producers' economic philosophy with its labor-cost theory and antimonopolist creed. From 1825 until the late eighties, together with the concept of self-help through co-operatives, they had furnished the ideological foundations of working-class movements in the United States. This economic philosophy, which represented the outlook of the lower middle class, instead of that of a job-conscious proletariat, made it possible, therefore, for labor reformers to participate along with farmers in radical movements that were based upon a similar philosophy that had been derived originally from working-class Locofocoism and elaborated on the basis of rural experience and subsequent intercourse with urban centers. Perhaps, as Henry David contends, antimonopolism was the peculiar program offered by the American workingman as his contribution to the realization of the "American dream." Only with the rise of modern trades unions after 1880 did wage earners come gradually to the view that they should work for their own craft interests independently of the farmers or the middle class. The story of the labor movement in the late eighties and early nineties centers upon the struggle between the new trades unionism and the older school of labor reform with its producers' philosophy that had united wage earner and

farmer in a common faith over six decades.

It was entirely normal, therefore, for the leaders of the farmers' alliances and for agrarian advocates of a third party to confer with Terence V. Powderly rather than with Samuel Gompers between 1889 and 1892. Unfortunately for the Populists, the swift decline of the Knights of Labor, champions of the older philosophy of American wage earners, made them an insufficient recruiting ground. The trades union leaders, on the other hand, apart from their job-conscious, autonomous outlook, were hardly conciliated by Populist preference for the leaders of the rival labor movement. Both factors, undoubtedly, motivated Samuel Gompers to write for the *North American Review*, just before the Omaha convention, that although labor would be friendlier to the People's Party than to any other, there could be no hope of a complete "unification of labor's forces in the field, farm, factory, and workshop." Because the Populists were largely "*employing* farmers" in contrast with the "*employed* farmers of the country districts or the mechanics and laborers of the industrial centers" Gompers persuaded his followers and the public that complete "coöperation or amalgamation of the wage-workers' organizations with the People's Party" was "impossible, because it is unnatural." The success of the Populists in recruiting a following from the ranks of organized labor depended, therefore, upon whether the wage earners' attachment for the older and more distinctively American philosophy of labor reform was greater than its loyalty to the newer, imported trades unionism. In 1892 the hold of the latter seems to have been stronger. After the panic of the following year had plunged labor into unemployment and acute distress, however, even Gompers wavered in his devotion to a strictly job-conscious, craft program. The American Federation of Labor actually moved toward a *de facto* alliance with Populism. The depression years, therefore, tended to force organized labor back into the older philosophy and justified making one more attempt to form a common front with the agrarian movement. This presented the Populists with their long-sought opportunity to recruit heavily from urban labor. It furnished the acid test of a radical creed based upon antimonopolism, the labor-cost theory of wealth, and belief in the common interests of all producers, which offered a limited but clearly defined economic collectivism as the goal of the farmer-labor alliance.

Perhaps because they have been preoccupied with interpretations derived from the older Turnerism, historians are just beginning to inquire into this neglected aspect of the Populist movement. When it is given full attention it will be found that the greatest problem of ideological conflict and adaptation produced by the attempted coalition did not develop out of a clash between Populism and the half-formulated philosophy of a shattered trades unionism. It occurred, instead, between the indigenous radicalism that Populism had inherited from decades of cross-fertilization between urban and agrarian radical movements, and an imported, proletarian Socialism which made its first great appeal to English-speaking wage earners in America in the depression-ridden nineties. At least some of the zeal with which the Populist national headquarters and Congressional delegation turned to free silver in 1895–1896 was the result of this far more irreconcilable conflict. The tendency of the strong antimonopoly bloc within the party to come to provisional terms with the Socialists on the basis of government ownership of all monopolies, which Henry D. Lloyd and the Nationalists supported, motivated some of the steamroller tactics with which Herman E. Taubeneck and Senator William V. Allen deprived the powerful antimonoplist-Nationalist-labor-and-Socialist element at the St. Louis convention of effective expression in 1896 and delivered the People's Party into the hands of the free-silver Democracy. This precipitated the withdrawal of the labor and left wing elements from all association with the Populists.

II. POPULIST IDEOLOGY: REVISIONISTS AND THEIR CRITICS

Richard Hofstadter: THE FOLKLORE OF POPULISM

Richard Hofstadter's work is the most renowned of the controversial revisionist studies which locate the root of the Populist ideology in a largely irrational and potentially dangerous psychology. In this selection the author describes Populism's simplistic economics, anti-Semitism, and conspiracy theory of history.

FOR A generation after the Civil War, a time of great economic exploitation and waste, grave social corruption and ugliness, the dominant note in American political life was complacency. Although dissenting minorities were always present, they were submerged by the overwhelming realities of industrial growth and continental settlement. The agitation of the Populists, which brought back to American public life a capacity for effective political indignation, marks the beginning of the end of this epoch. In the short run the Populists did not get what they wanted, but they released the flow of protest and criticism that swept through American political affairs from the 1890's to the beginning of the first World War.

Where contemporary intellectuals gave the Populists a perfunctory and disdainful hearing, later historians have freely recognized their achievements and frequently overlooked their limitations. Modern liberals, finding the Populists' grievances valid, their programs suggestive, their motives creditable, have usually spoken of the Populist episode in the spirit of Vachel Lindsay's bombastic rhetoric:

Prairie avenger, mountain lion,
Bryan, Bryan, Bryan, Bryan,
Gigantic troubadour, speaking
  like a siege gun,
Smashing Plymouth Rock with his boulders
  from the West.

There is indeed much that is good and usable in our Populist past. While the Populist tradition had defects that have been too much neglected, it does not follow that the virtues claimed for it are all fictitious. Populism was the first modern political movement of practical importance in the United States to insist that the federal government has some responsibility for the common weal; indeed, it was the first such movement to attack seriously the problems created by industrialism. The complaints and demands and prophetic denunciations of the Populists stirred the latent liberalism in many Americans and startled many conservatives into a new flexibility. Most of the "radical" reforms in the Populist program proved in later years to be either harmless or useful. In at least one important area of American life a few Populist leaders in the South attempted something profoundly radical and humane — to build a popular movement that would

From *The Age of Reform* by Richard Hofstadter, pp. 60–81. © Copyright 1955 by Richard Hofstadter. Reprinted by permission of Alfred A. Knopf, Inc.

cut across the old barriers of race — until persistent use of the Negro bogy distracted their following. To discuss the broad ideology of the Populists does them some injustice, for it was in their concrete programs that they added most constructively to our political life, and in their more general picture of the world that they were most credulous and vulnerable. Moreover, any account of the fallibility of Populist thinking that does not acknowledge the stress and suffering out of which that thinking emerged will be seriously remiss. But anyone who enlarges our portrait of the Populist tradition is likely to bring out some unseen blemishes. In the books that have been written about the Populist movement, only passing mention has been made of its significant provincialism; little has been said of its relations with nativism and nationalism; nothing has been said of its tincture of anti-Semitism.

The Populist impulse expressed itself in a set of notions that represent what I have called the "soft" side of agrarianism. These notions, which appear with regularity in the political literature, must be examined if we are to re-create for ourselves the Populist spirit. To extract them from the full context of the polemical writings in which they appeared is undoubtedly to oversimplify them; even to name them in any language that comes readily to the historian of ideas is perhaps to suggest that they had a formality and coherence that in reality they clearly lacked. But since it is less feasible to have no labels than to have somewhat too facile ones, we may enumerate the dominant themes in Populist ideology as these: the idea of a golden age; the concept of natural harmonies; the dualistic version of social struggles; the conspiracy theory of history; and the doctrine of the primacy of money. The last of these I will touch

upon in connection with the free-silver issue. Here I propose to analyze the others, and to show how they were nurtured by the traditions of the agrarian myth.

The utopia of the Populists was in the past, not the future. According to the agrarian myth, the health of the state was proportionate to the degree to which it was dominated by the agricultural class, and this assumption pointed to the superiority of an earlier age. The Populists looked backward with longing to the lost agrarian Eden, to the republican America of the early years of the nineteenth century in which there were few millionaires and, as they saw it, no beggars, when the laborer had excellent prospects and the farmer had abundance, when statesmen still responded to the mood of the people and there was no such thing as the money power. What they meant — though they did not express themselves in such terms — was that they would like to restore the conditions prevailing before the development of industrialism and the commercialization of agriculture. It should not be surprising that they inherited the traditions of Jacksonian democracy, that they revived the old Jacksonian cry: "Equal Rights for All, Special Privileges for None," or that most of the slogans of 1896 echoed the battle cries of 1836. General James B. Weaver, the Populist candidate for the presidency in 1892, was an old Democrat and Free-Soiler, born during the days of Jackson's battle with the United States Bank, who drifted into the Greenback movement after a short spell as a Republican, and from there to Populism. His book, *A Call to Action*, published in 1892, drew up an indictment of the business corporation which reads like a Jacksonian polemic. Even in those hopeful early days of the People's Party, Weaver projected no grandiose plans for the future, but lamented the course of recent history, the growth of economic oppression, and the emergence of great contrasts of wealth and poverty, and called upon his readers to do "All in [their] power to arrest the alarming tendencies of our times."

Nature, as the agrarian tradition had it, was beneficent. The United States was abundantly endowed with rich land and rich resources, and the "natural" consequence of such an endowment should be the prosperity of the people. If the people failed to enjoy prosperity, it must be because of a harsh and arbitrary intrusion of human greed and error. "Hard times, then," said one popular writer, "as well as the bankruptcies, enforced idleness, starvation, and the crime, misery, and moral degradation growing out of conditions like the present, being unnatural, not in accordance with, or the result of any natural law, must be attributed to that kind of unwise and pernicious legislation which history proves to have produced similar results in all ages of the world. It is the mission of the age to correct these errors in human legislation, to adopt and establish policies and systems, in accord with, rather than in opposition to divine law." In assuming a lush natural order whose workings were being deranged by human laws, Populist writers were again drawing on the Jacksonian tradition, whose spokesmen also had pleaded for a proper obedience to "natural" laws as a prerequisite of social justice.

Somewhat akin to the notion of the beneficence of nature was the idea of a natural harmony of interests among the productive classes. To the Populist mind there was no fundamental conflict between the farmer and the worker, between the toiling people and the small businessman. While there might be cor-

rupt individuals in any group, the underlying interests of the productive majority were the same; predatory behavior existed only because it was initiated and underwritten by a small parasitic minority in the highest places of power. As opposed to the idea that society consists of a number of different and frequently clashing interests — the social pluralism expressed, for instance, by Madison in the *Federalist* — the Populists adhered, less formally to be sure, but quite persistently, to a kind of social dualism: although they knew perfectly well that society was composed of a number of classes, for all practical purposes only one simple division need be considered. There were two nations. "It it a struggle," said Sockless Jerry Simpson, "between the robbers and the robbed." "There are but two sides in the conflict that is being waged in this country today," declared a Populist manifesto. "On the one side are the allied hosts of monopolies, the money power, great trusts and railroad corporations, who seek the enactment of laws to benefit them and impoverish the people. On the other are the farmers, laborers, merchants, and all other people who produce wealth and bear the burdens of taxation. ... Between these two there is no middle ground." "On the one side," said Bryan in his famous speech against the repeal of tthe Sherman Silver Purchase Act, "stand the corporate interests of the United States, the moneyed interests, aggregated wealth and capital, imperious, arrogant, compassionless. . . . On the other side stand an unnumbered throng, those who gave to the Democratic party a name and for whom it has assumed to speak." The people versus the interests, the public versus the plutocrats, the toiling multitude versus the money power — in various phrases this central antagonism was

expressed. From this simple social classi-
fication it seemed to follow that once the
techniques of misleading the people were
exposed, victory over the money power
ought to be easily accomplished, for in
sheer numbers the people were overwhelming. "There is no power on earth
that can defeat us," said General Weaver
during the optimistic days of the campaign of 1892. "It is a fight between labor
and capital, and labor is in the vast
majority."

The problems that faced the Populists
assumed a delusive simplicity: the victory over injustice, the solution for all
social ills, was concentrated in the crusade against a single, relatively small but
immensely strong interest, the money
power. "With the destruction of the
money power," said Senator Peffer, "the
death knell of gambling in grain and
other commodities will be sounded; for
the business of the worst men on earth
will have been broken up, and the main-
stay of the gamblers removed. It will be
an easy matter, after the greater spoils-
men have been shorn of their power, to
clip the wings of the little ones. Once we
get rid of the men who hold the country
by the throat, the parasites can be easily
removed." Since the old political parties
were the primary means by which the
people were kept wandering in the wilderness, the People's Party advocates insisted, only a new and independent
political party could do this essential job.
As the silver question became more
prominent and the idea of a third party
faded, the need for a monolithic solution
became transmuted into another form:
there was only one *issue* upon which the
money power could really be beaten and
this was the money issue. "When we
have restored the money of the Constitution," said Bryan in his Cross of Gold
speech, "all other necessary reforms will

be possible; but . . . until this is done
there is no other reform that can be accomplished."

While the conditions of victory were
thus made to appear simple, they did not
always appear easy, and it would be misleading to imply that the tone of Populistic thinking was uniformly optimistic.
Often, indeed, a deep-lying vein of
anxiety showed through. The very sharp-
ness of the struggle, as the Populists ex-
perienced it, the alleged absence of compromise solutions and of intermediate
groups in the body politic, the brutality
and desperation that were imputed to
the plutocracy — all these suggested that
failure of the people to win the final
contest peacefully could result only in a
total victory for the plutocrats and total
extinction of democratic institutions, possibly after a period of bloodshed and
anarchy. "We are nearing a serious
crisis," declared Weaver. "If the present
strained relations between wealth owners
and wealth producers continue much
longer they will ripen into frightful disaster. This universal discontent must be
quickly interpreted and its causes removed." "We meet," said the Populist
platform of 1892, "in the midst of a nation
brought to the verge of moral, political,
and material ruin. Corruption dominates
the ballot-box, the Legislatures, the Congress, and touches even the ermine of the
bench. The people are demoralized . . .
The newspapers are largely subsidized or
muzzled, public opinion silenced, business prostrated, homes covered with
mortgages, labor impoverished, and the
land concentrating in the hands of the
capitalists. The urban workmen are denied the right to organize for self-protec-
tion, imported pauperized labor beats
down their wages, a hireling standing
army, unrecognized by our laws, is established to shoot them down, and they are

rapidly degenerating into European conditions. The fruits of the toil of millions are boldly stolen to build up colossal fortunes for a few, unprecedented in the history of mankind; and the possessors of these, in turn, despise the Republic and endanger liberty." Such conditions forboded "the destruction of civilization, or the establishment of an absolute despotism."

The common fear of an impending apocalypse had its most striking articulation in Ignatius Donnelly's fantastic novel *Cæsar's Column*. This book, published under a pseudonym, was a piece of visionary writing, possibly inspired by the success a few years earlier of Bellamy's utopian romance *Looking Backward*, which called forth a spate of imitators during the last decade of the century. Praised by leading members of the Populist movement and by persons as diverse as Cardinal Gibbons, George Cary Eggleston, Frances E. Willard, and Julian Hawthorne, *Cæsar's Column* became one of the most widely read books of the early nineties. Donnelly's was different from the other utopias. Although in its anticlimactic conclusion it did describe a utopia in a remote spot of Africa, the main story portrayed a sadistic antiutopia arrived at, as it were, by standing Bellamy on his head. The idea seems to have occurred to Donnelly in a moment of great discouragement at the close of the unusually corrupt Minnesota legislative session of 1889, when he was struck with the thought of what might come to be if the worst tendencies of current society were projected a century into the future. The story takes place in the year 1988, missing by four years the date of the more recent anti-utopia of George Orwell, with which it invites comparison, though not on literary grounds.

Donnelly's hero and narrator is a stranger, a shepherd of Swiss extraction living in the state of Uganda, Africa, who visits New York and reports his adventures in a series of letters. New York is a center of technological marvels much like Bellamy's. The stranger approaches it in an airship, finds it lit so brightly that its life goes on both night and day. Its streets are covered with roofs of glass; underneath them is the city's subway system, with smokeless and noiseless electric trains to which passengers are lowered by electric elevators. Its air-conditioned hotels are capped by roof-top restaurants serving incredible luxuries, where "star-eyed maidens . . . wonder half seen amid the foliage, like the houris in the Mohammedan's heaven."

This sybaritic life is supported at the cost of great mass suffering, and conceals a fierce social struggle. The world of 1988 is governed by an inner council of plutocratic leaders who stop at nothing to crush potential opposition. They keep in their hire a fleet of "Demons," operators of dirigibles carrying poison-gas bombs, whose aid they are ready to use at any sign of popular opposition. The people themselves have become equally ruthless — "brutality above had produced brutality below." The farmers are "no longer the honest yeomanry who had filled, in the old time, the armies of Washington, and Jackson, and Grant, and Sherman . . . but their brutalized descendants — fierce serfs — cruel and bloodthirsty peasants." The brunt of the social struggle, however, is borne by the urban laborers, a polyglot, silent mass of sullen, underfed humanity. The traveler from Uganda learns in a conversation (documented by Donnelly with real articles from current magazines) that as early as 1889 many writers had warned against the potentialities of this state of affairs. It was not an inevitable development, but greed and stupidity had kept the ruling classes from heeding such prophets of disaster. Rapacious business methods, the bribery of voters, the exploitation of workers and farmers by the plutocracy, had gone unchecked until the end of the nineteenth century, when the proletariat had rebelled. The rebellion had been put down by the farmers, not yet completely expelled by mortgage foreclosures from their position as property-owners and businessmen. Now that the farmers too are destroyed as a prop of the existing order, the rulers rely solely upon the bomb, the dirigible, and a mercenary army.

The convolutions of Donnelly's plot, which includes two tasteless love stories, do little more than entitle the book to be called a novel, and the work is full of a kind of suppressed lasciviousness that one finds often in popular writing of the period. At the climax of the story, the secret revolutionary organization, the Brotherhood of Destruction, after buying off the "Demons," revolts and begins an incredible round of looting and massacre which may have been modeled on the French Revolutionary Terror but makes it seem pale and bloodless in comparison. Some members of the governing class are forced to build a pyre on which they are then burned. There is so much carnage that the disposal of the bodies becomes an immense sanitary problem. Cæsar, one of the three leaders (who is himself beheaded in the end), commands that the corpses be piled up and covered with cement to form a gigantic pyramidal column as a monument to the uprising. The city is finally burned, but a saving remnant of decent folk escapes in a dirigible to the African mountains, where under the guidance of an elite of intellectuals they form a Christian socialist state in which the Populist program for land, transportation, and finance becomes a reality and interest is illegal.

Doubtless this fantasy was meant to say what would happen if the warnings of the reformers and the discontents of the people went unheard and unalleviated. Far more ominous, however, than any of the vivid and hideous predictions of the book is the sadistic and nihilistic spirit in which it was written. It is perhaps a childish book, but in the middle of the twentieth century it seems anything but laughable: it affords a frightening glimpse into the ugly potential of frustrated popular revolt. When *Cæsar's Column* appeared, the reform movement in America had not yet made a dent upon the torments and oppressions that were felt by a large portion of the people. In some men the situation fostered a feeling of desperation, and Donnelly's was a desperate work. It came at a moment when the threat of a social apocalypse seemed to many people not at all remote, and it remains even now a nettlesome if distinctly minor prophetic book.

History as Conspiracy

Both sides of Donnelly's struggle, the Council of governing plutocrats and the Brotherhood of Destruction, are significantly portrayed as secret organizations — this despite the fact that the Brotherhood has millions of members. There was something about the Populist imagination that loved the secret plot and the conspiratorial meeting. There was in fact a widespread Populist idea that all American history since the Civil War could be understood as a sustained conspiracy of the international money power.

The pervasiveness of this way of looking at things may be attributed to the common feeling that farmers and workers were not simply oppressed but oppressed deliberately, consciously, and with wanton malice by "the interests." It would of course be misleading to imply that the Populists stand alone in thinking of the events of their time as the results of a conspiracy. This kind of thinking frequently occurs when political and social antagonisms are sharp. Certain audiences are especially susceptible to it — particularly, I believe, those who have attained only a low level of education, whose access to information is poor, and who are so completely shut out from access to the centers of power that they feel themselves completely deprived of self-defense and subjected to unlimited manipulation by those who wield power. There are, moreover, certain types of popular movements of dissent that offer special opportunities to agitators with paranoid tendencies, who are able to make a vocational asset out of their psychic disturbances. Such persons have an opportunity to impose their own style of thought upon the movements they lead. It would of course be misleading to imply that there are no such things as conspiracies in history. Anything that partakes of political strategy may need, for a time at least, an element of secrecy, and is thus vulnerable to being dubbed conspiratorial. Corruption itself has the character of conspiracy. In this sense the Crédit Mobilier was a conspiracy, as was the Teapot Dome affair. If we tend to be too condescending to the Populists at this point, it may be necessary to remind ourselves that they had seen so much bribery and corruption, particularly on the part of the railroads, that they had before them a convincing model of the management of affairs through conspiratorial behavior. Indeed, what makes conspiracy theories so widely acceptable is that they usually contain a germ of truth. But there is a great difference between locating conspiracies in history and saying that history *is*, in effect, a conspiracy, between singling out those conspiratorial acts that do on occasion occur and weaving a vast fabric of social explanation out of nothing but skeins of evil plots.

When conspiracies do not exist it is necessary for those who think in this fashion to invent them. Among the most celebrated instances in modern history are the forgery of the Protocols of the Elders of Zion and the grandiose fabrication under Stalin's regime of the Trotzky-it-Bukharinite-Zinovievite center. These inventions were cynical. In the history of American political controversy there is a tradition of conspiratorial accusations which seem to have been sincerely believed. Jefferson appears really to have believed, at one time, that the Federalists were conspiring to re-establish monarchy. Some Federalists believed that the Jeffersonians were conspiring to subvert Christianity. The movement to annex Texas and the war with Mexico were alleged by many Northerners to be a slaveholders' conspiracy. The early Republican leaders, including Lincoln, charged that there was a conspiracy on the part of Stephen A. Douglas to make slavery a nationwide institution. Such pre-Civil War parties as the Know-Nothing and Anti-Masonic movements were based almost entirely upon conspiratorial ideology. The Nye Committee, years ago, tried to prove that our entry into the first World War was the work of a conspiracy of bankers and munitions-makers. And now not only our entry into the second World War, but the entire history of the past twenty years or so is being given the color of conspiracy by the cranks and political fakirs of our own age.

Nevertheless, when these qualifications have been taken into account, it remains true that Populist thought showed an unusually strong tendency to account for relatively impersonal events in highly personal terms. An overwhelming sense of grievance does not find satisfactory expression in impersonal explanations, except among those with a well-developed tradition of intellectualism. It is the city, after all, that is the home of intellectual complexity. The farmer lived in isolation from the great world in which his fate was actually decided. He was accused of being unusually suspicious, and certainly his situation, trying as it was, made thinking in impersonal terms difficult. Perhaps the rural middle-class leaders of Populism (this was a movement of farmers, but it was not led by farmers) had more to do than the farmer himself with the cast of Populist thinking. At any rate, Populist thought often carries one into a world in which the simple virtues and unmitigated villainies of a rural melodrama have been projected on a national and even an international scale. In Populist thought the farmer is not a speculating businessman, victimized by the risk economy of which he is a part, but rather a wounded yeoman, preyed upon by those who are alien to the life of the folkish virtue. A villain was needed, marked with the unmistakable stigmata of the villains of melodrama, and the more remote he was from the familiar scene, the more plausibly his villainies could be exaggerated.

It was not enough to say that a conspiracy of the money power against the common people was going on. It had been going on ever since the Civil War. It was not enough to say that it stemmed from Wall Street. It was international: it stemmed from Lombard Street. In his preamble to the People's Party platform of 1892, a succinct, official expression of Populist views, Ignatius Donnelly asserted:

A vast conspiracy against mankind has been organized on two continents, and it is rapidly taking possession of the world. If not met and overthrown at once it forebodes terrible social convulsions, the destruction of civilization, or the establishment of an absolute despotism.

A manifesto of 1895, signed by fifteen outstanding leaders of the People's Party, declared:

As early as 1865–66 a conspiracy was entered into between the gold gamblers of Europe and America. . . . For nearly thirty years these conspirators have kept the people quarreling over less important matters while they have pursued with unrelenting zeal their one central purpose. . . . Every device of treachery, every resource of statecraft, and every artifice known to the secret cabals of the international gold ring are being made use of to deal a blow to the prosperity of the people and the financial and commercial independence of the country.

The financial argument behind the conspiracy theory was simple enough. Those who owned bonds wanted to be paid not in a common currency but in gold, which was at a premium; those who lived by lending money wanted as high a premium as possible to be put on their commodity by increasing its scarcity. The panics, depressions, and bankruptcies caused by their policies only added to their wealth; such catastrophes offered opportunities to engross the wealth of others through business consolidations and foreclosures. Hence the interests actually relished and encouraged hard times. The Greenbackers had long since popularized this argument, insisting that an adequate legal-tender currency would break the monopoly of the "Shylocks." Their demand for $50 of circulating medium per capita, still in the air when the People's Party arose, was rapidly replaced by the less "radical" demand for free coinage of silver. But what both the Greenbackers and free-silverites held in common was the idea that the contraction of currency was a deliberate squeeze, the result of a long-range plot of the "Anglo-American Gold Trust." Wherever one turns in the Populist literature of the nineties one can find this conspiracy theory expressed. It is in the Populist newspapers, the proceedings of the silver conventions, the immense pamphlet literature broadcast by the American Bimetallic League, the Congressional debates over money; it is elaborated in such popular books as Mrs. S. E. V. Emery's *Seven Financial Conspiracies Which Have Enslaved the American People* or Gordon Clark's *Shylock: as Banker, Bondholder, Corruptionist, Conspirator.*

Mrs. Emery's book, first published in 1887, and dedicated to "the enslaved people of a dying republic," achieved great circulation, especially among the Kansas Populists. According to Mrs. Emery, the United States had been an economic Garden of Eden in the period before the Civil War. The fall of man had dated from the war itself, when "the money kings of Wall Street" determined that they could take advantage of the wartime necessities of their fellow men by manipulating the currency. "Controlling it, they could inflate or depress the business of the country at pleasure, they could send the warm life current through the channels of trade, dispensing peace, happiness, and prosperity, or they could check its flow, and completely paralyze the industries of the country." With this great power for good in their hands, the Wall Street men preferred to do evil. Lincoln's war policy of issuing greenbacks presented them with the dire threat of an adequate supply of currency.

So the Shylocks gathered in convention and "perfected" a conspiracy to create a demand for their gold. The remainder of the book was a recital of a series of seven measures passed between 1862 and 1875 which were alleged to be a part of this continuing conspiracy, the total effect of which was to contract the currency of the country further and further until finally it squeezed the industry of the country like a hoop of steel.

Mrs. Emery's rhetoric left no doubt of the sustained purposefulness of this scheme — described as "villainous robbery," and as having been "secured through the most soulless strategy." She was most explicit about the so-called "crime of 1873," the demonetization of silver, giving a fairly full statement of the standard greenback-silverite myth concerning that event. As they had it, an agent of the Bank of England, Ernest Seyd by name, had come to the United States in 1872 with $500,000 with which he had bought enough support in Congress to secure the passage of the demonetization measure. This measure was supposed to have greatly increased the value of American four per cent bonds held by British capitalists by making it necessary to pay them in gold only. To it Mrs. Emery attributed the panic of 1873, its bankruptcies, and its train of human disasters: "Murder, insanity, suicide, divorce, drunkenness and all forms of immorality and crime have increased from that day to this in the most appalling ratio."

"Coin" Harvey, the author of the most popular single document of the whole currency controversy, *Coin's Financial School,* also published a novel, *A Tale of Two Nations,* in which the conspiracy theory of history was incorporated into a melodramatic tale. In this story the powerful English banker Baron Rothe plans to bring about the demonetization of silver in the United States, in part for his own aggrandizement but also to prevent the power of the United States from outstripping that of England. He persuades an American Senator (probably John Sherman, the *bête noire* of the silverites) to cooperate in using British gold in a campaign against silver. To be sure that the work is successful, he also sends to the United States a relative and ally, one Rogasner, who stalks through the story like the villains in the plays of Dion Boucicault, muttering to himself such remarks as "I am here to destroy the United States — Cornwallis could not have done more. For the wrongs and insults, for the glory of my own country, I will bury the knife deep into the heart of this nation." Against the plausibly drawn background of the corruption of the Grant administration, Rogasner proceeds to buy up the American Congress and suborn American professors of economics to testify for gold. He also falls in love with a proud American beauty, but his designs on her are foiled because she loves a handsome young silver Congressman from Nebraska who bears a striking resemblance to William Jennings Bryan!

One feature of the Populist conspiracy theory that has been generally overlooked is its frequent link with a kind of rhetorical anti-Semitism. The slight current of anti-Semitism that existed in the United States before the 1890's had been associated with problems of money and credit. During the closing years of the century it grew noticeably. While the jocose and rather heavy-handed anti-Semitism that can be found in Henry Adams's letters of the 1890's shows that this prejudice existed outside Populist literature, it was chiefly Populist writers who expressed that identification of the Jew with the usurer and the "interna-

tional gold ring" which was the cental treme of the American anti-Semitism of the age. The omnipresent symbol of Shylock can hardly be taken in itself as evidence of anti-Semitism, but the frequent references to the House of Rothschild make it clear that for many silverites the Jew was an organic part of the conspiracy theory of history. Coin Harvey's Baron Rothe was clearly meant to be Rothschild; his Rogasner (Ernest Seyd?) was a dark figure out of the coarsest anti-Semitic tradition. "You are very wise in your way," Rogasner is told at the climax of the tale, "the commercial way, inbred through generations. The politic, scheming, devious way, inbred through generations also." One of the cartoons in the effectively illustrated *Coin's Financial School* showed a map of the world dominated by the tentacles of an octopus at the site of the British Isles, labeled: "Rothschilds." In Populist demonology, anti-Semitism and Anglophobia went hand in hand.

The note of anti-Semitism was often sounded openly in the campaign for silver. A representative of the New Jersey Grange, for instance, did not hesitate to warn the members of the Second National Silver Convention of 1892 to watch out for political candidates who represented "Wall Street, and the Jews of Europe." Mary E. Lease described Grover Cleveland as "the agent of Jewish bankers and British gold." Donnelly represented the leader of the governing Council of plutocrats in *Cæsar's Column*, one Prince Cabano, as a powerful Jew, born Jacob Isaacs; one of the triumvirate who led the Brotherhood of Destruction is also an exiled Russian Jew, who flees from the apocalyptic carnage with a hundred million dollars which he intends to use to "revive the ancient splendors of the Jewish race, in the midst of the ruins of the world." One of the more elaborate documents of the conspiracy school traced the power of the Rothschilds over America to a transaction between Hugh McCulloch, Secretary of the Treasury under Lincoln and Johnson, and Baron James Rothschild. "The most direful part of this business between Rothschild and the United States Treasury was not the loss of money, even by hundreds of millions. It was the resignation of the country itself into the hands of England, as England had long been resigned into the hands of her Jews."

Such rhetoric, which became common currency in the movement, later passed beyond Populism into the larger stream of political protest. By the time the campaign of 1896 arrived, an Associated Press reporter noticed as "one of the striking things" about the Populist convention at St. Louis "the extraordinary hatred of the Jewish race. It is not possible to go into any hotel in the city without hearing the most bitter denunciation of the Jews as a class and of the particular Jews who happen to have prospered in the world." This report may have been somewhat overdone, but the identification of the silver cause with anti-Semitism did become close enough for Bryan to have to pause in the midst of his campaign to explain to the Jewish Democrats of Chicago that in denouncing the policies of the Rothschilds he and his silver friends were "not attacking a race; we are attacking greed and avarice which know no race or religion."

It would be easy to misstate the character of Populist anti-Semitism or to exaggerate its intensity. For Populist anti-Semitism was entirely verbal. It was a mode of expression, a rhetorical style, not a tactic or a program. It did not lead to exclusion laws, much less to riots or pogroms. There were, after all, relatively few Jews in the United States in the late 1880's and early 1890's, most of them remote from the areas of Populist strength. It is one thing, however, to say that this prejudice did not go beyond a certain symbolic usage, quite another to say that a people's choice of symbols is of no significance. Populist anti-Semitism does have its importance — chiefly as a symptom of a certain ominous credulity in the Populist mind. It is not too much to say that the Greenback-Populist tradition activated most of what we have of modern popular anti-Semitism in the United States. From Thaddeus Stevens and Coin Harvey to Father Coughlin, and from Brooks and Henry Adams to Ezra Pound, there has been a curiously persistent linkage between anti-Semitism and money and credit obsessions. A full history of modern anti-Semitism in the United States would reveal, I believe, its substantial Populist lineage, but it may be sufficient to point out here that neither the informal connection between Bryan and the Klan in the twenties nor Thomas E. Watson's conduct in the Leo Frank case were altogether fortuitous. And Henry Ford's notorious anti-Semitism of the 1920's, along with his hatred of "Wall Street," were the foibles of a Michigan farm boy who had been liberally exposed to Populist notions.

Norman Pollack: A CRITIQUE OF THE HOFSTADTER THESIS

Norman Pollack, one of the historians who arose to challenge the revisionists' interpretation of the Populist movement, here focuses exclusively on Hofstadter's The Age of Reform. *Particularly objectionable to Pollack is Hofstadter's "consensus" approach to Populism.*

RICHARD HOFSTADTER announces at the beginning of *The Age of Reform* that he will present a new interpretation of American reform movements since 1890 "from the perspective of our time.". . . But what justification can there be in risking the possibility of simply reflecting prevailing sentiments by writing "from the perspective of our own time"? Hofstadter gives as his reason the need to appraise critically what he calls "the New Deal experience," that is, the effect of New Deal scholarship upon the interpretation of these reform movements:

Our conception of Populism and Progressivism has in fact been intimately bound up with the New Deal experience . . . . The views, therefore, of Populism and Progressivism that one finds in histories written during and shortly after the New Deal era bear inevitably the stamp of this second wave of reform.

In justifying his perspective, however, Hofstadter neglects to tell us what these New Deal books are, and, as a matter of fact, the important books on Populism were written well *before* the New Deal. . . . The result is that Hofstadter, by failing to make clear what he criticizes, can offer a new interpretation without refuting the older.

What are the grounds for Hofstadter's dissatisfaction with interpretations "bound up with the New Deal experience"? He provides the following explanation:

I find that I have been critical of the Populist-Progressive tradition — more so than I would have been had I been writing such a study fifteen years ago. I say critical, but not hostile, for I am criticizing largely from within . . . . The flow of criticism between conservatives and liberals in the United States has been somewhat blocked, with the consequence that men on both sides have grown excessively complacent about their intellectual positions. In the absence of a formidable and reasoned body of conservative criticism, liberals have been driven, for that exercise of the mind which intellectuals seek, to self-criticism, which has been of less value to them than powerful and searching opposition.

This justification does not seem altogether plausible, for it is hard to accept the notion that something happened in those "fifteen years" which changed the validity of historical conclusions. Moreover, can it seriously be asserted that there are no objective grounds upon which liberals can criticize conservatives, and that the liberal intellectual has only one valid task, to keep in condition by exercising his mind on self-criticism? The notion that material and ideological differences are nonexistent in American society leads to the conclusion that there

From Norman Pollack, "Hofstadter on Populism: A Critique of 'The Age of Reform,'" *Journal of Southern History*, Vol. XXVI (November 1960), pp. 478–500. Copyright 1960 by the Southern Historical Association. Reprinted by permission of the Managing Editor.

is nothing really left to criticize. It is suggested, therefore, that Hofstadter's basic methodological assumption is his consensus thesis: Consensus upon capitalist values characterizes the basic pattern of American development.

Hofstadter subtly invokes the consensus thesis in his definition of Populism, in which he includes characteristics so diverse as to deny that the movement had any cohesive force. In fact, his definition is so general that it divorces Populism from its historical context.

By "Populism" [he writes] I do not mean only the People's (or Populist) Party of the 1890's; for I consider the Populist Party to be merely a heightened expression, at a particular moment of time, of a kind of popular impulse that is endemic in American political culture . . . that expressed the discontents of a great many farmers and businessmen with the economic changes of the late nineteenth century . . . . I believe that Populist thinking has survived in our own time, partly as an undercurrent of provincial resentments, popular and "democratic" rebelliousness and suspiciousness, and nativism.

From this definition three noteworthy consequences follow: (1) The inclusion of businessmen already colors the movement by orienting it to profit-making; (2) the addition of nativism gives the movement from the start the appearance of irrational protest, rather than of protest based upon economic grievances; and (3) the description of Populism as a "popular impulse that is endemic in American political culture" implies a recurrent theme, rather than a specific movement in a given historical context. This lack of concreteness allows Hofstadter to support the consensus thesis by treating the whole course of American history in terms of "endemic" impulses. Thus, the consensus thesis is established on an *ahistorical* basis; and the result

can only be the assumption that American society has always existed in a state of equilibrium. But how can protest even occur given an equilibrium framework? By definition, the explanation must lie in factors external to the system; or, and here is the significant loophole, such protest must be taken as a presumption of irrationality.

Yet Hofstadter does offer a way to treat movements which fall outside the consensus framework; he denies that they are outside. Since the very existence of protest movements creates a suspicion that the consensus thesis is invalid, it is not really sufficient to dismiss these movements as irrational; rather, it is necessary to assert that, while irrational, they actually reflect deep-down the basic consensus. Hence, irrational protest must be interpreted merely as a more vociferous expression of consensus. At a later point it will be seen that Hofstadter does precisely this. He considers the Populists to be irrational, while at the same time he regards them as oriented to capitalism. The result is that protest, even when it occurs, cannot be regarded as protest against the system; protest *qua* protest is inadmissible.

In an examination of *The Age of Reform* it becomes apparent that the entire analysis of Populism is built upon Hofstadter's selection of five dominant themes in Populist ideology.[1] This is a particularly weak foundation because it considers the movement only on the ideological level, eliminating at the outset historical and sociological factors. This procedure, moreover, heightens the possibility of an arbitrary selection of mate-

[1] The five themes are "the idea of a golden age; the concept of natural harmonies; the dualistic version of social struggles; the conspiracy theory of history; and the doctrine of the primacy of money." . . .

rial because statements have been removed from the historical context in which they occurred. Once statements become divorced in this way, they can be used to support any thesis; or, as is more generally true here, they can be made to appear ridiculous. A systematic treatment of Populist economic grievances would provide a necessary correction to this bias, but this is accorded a negligible role in Hofstadter's analysis.

The most important objection that can be raised to Hofstadter's procedure, however, concerns the actual organization of the five themes in the ideology. With the introduction of these themes Hofstadter conveys the impression that they represent an examination of the "political literature" in order "to re-create for ourselves the Populist spirit." Hence, he appears to be merely categorizing these themes "from the full context of the polemical writings"; or, stated more precisely, a content analysis of Populist thought yields these five themes. Thus far no internal relationship between the themes is specified, nor presumably does one exist. The only relationship one would expect to find stems from their common source, Populism itself; but the assumption is that the relationship is *unplanned*. Hofstadter's procedure merely calls for a recombination of the themes to form an image of the "Populist spirit."

It should be noted, however, that Hofstadter does not follow this procedure. On the contrary, these themes have been carefully constructed so as to contribute to an overall impression. That is, they exhibit a planned internal relationship which unfolds in this manner: Each time a theme is allegedly established, it then sets the stage for the following theme, and so on until an image is created. Specifically, the first three themes assert the essential irrationality of Populism which, when accepted, then introduces the most likely manifestation of irrationality — belief in a conspiracy theory of history. This leads directly to the assertion that the Populists were anti-Semitic. By this time the reader is so convinced that Populism was not a response to actual conditions that the final point is easily made: Populist leadership was opportunistic, and the movement really expressed in an irrational fashion a basic consensus. The nature of Populism thereby becomes a drive for higher status and a larger share of the national wealth. The result is a highly manipulative situation in which the reader is carried along to an inevitable conclusion — protest movements are merely manifestations of the "status revolution."

If Hofstadter had specified this internal relationship from the start, then the test for evaluating his total work would take the form of examining each theme. . . . Thus, it becomes necessary to examine each level of the analysis in order to show that the move to succeeding levels is unwarranted.

Hofstadter begins his whole discussion of Populist ideology with the sentence, "The utopia of the Populists was in the past, not the future." Thus, from the start Populism is considered a movement of irrational protest. Not only is it utopian, but it is retrogressively utopian; for the "Populists looked backward with longing to the lost agrarian Eden . . . ." Here Hofstadter makes the candid admismission, *"though they did not express themselves in such terms"* they looked backward because they wanted "to restore the conditions prevailing before the development of industrialism and the commercialization of agriculture." The evidence for this important contention is inadequate — three Populist works in all, and each inappropriately used because their presentation does not show that Populism resisted social change. By Hofstadter's own admission these items merely call attention to the fact that concentration of wealth, large numbers of tramps, and an unresponsive political system did not exist, for example, in Andrew Jackson's time to the extent that they were present during the industrial transformation. Hence, simply because James B. Weaver, Populist candidate for the presidency in 1892, urged that "the alarming tendencies of our times" be arrested, it does not necessarily follow that he wanted to restore an earlier age.

Hofstadter's line of reasoning on this point raises several questions. First, does he deny that the Populist charge is correct, that conditions were in fact different in Jackson's time? Second, if it is correct, does the fact of its expression necessarily make it utopian? While Hofstadter's evidence neither proves nor disproves the charge of utopianism, the charge is itself significant for its implications. Unless the Populists viewed conditions of their own time as no more unjust than in earlier periods, and, further, unless they were willing to acquiesce in these conditions, they can be dismissed as retrogressively utopian. Hofstadter's view here appears to be a carry-over from his own methodological assumptions. He objects to the Populists' attempt to place their problems in historical perspective, thereby suggesting that a historical approach is itself utopian — precisely because by definition it looks backward.

But a more significant implication derives from the charge of utopianism. *Populist goals were unrealizable and impractical.* It follows that Populism did not advocate concrete measures to correct specific abuses, nor did it criticize the very nature of the social system. It

was only trying "to restore the conditions prevailing before the development of industrialism and the commercialization of agriculture." Thus, the argument is designed to support the consensus thesis as well as to suggest irrationality, because the Populists are regarded as yearning for an older society, not criticizing the existing one. And of the two, a nostalgic perspective, even if it implies some reservations concerning the status quo, is more consistent with the consensus thesis than is criticism of the society.

Hofstadter concludes his discussion of utopianism with what he regards as the basis for this retrogressive outlook, the belief that "Nature . . . was beneficent." That is, the Populists felt that American natural wealth had the potential to create abundance, but "If the people failed to enjoy prosperity, it must be because of a harsh and arbitrary intrusion of human greed and error." They assumed "a lush natural order whose workings were being deranged by human laws." If the issue is restated without trying to make the Populists appear ridiculous through such overstatements as "lush natural order," their position becomes the following: The material wealth of America had the potential to create prosperity throughout the society if it was equitably distributed or administered. Yet, this did not happen. Why? Because, contended Populism, human beings are responsible through control of legislation for transforming society into a highly inequitable system.

Hofstadter seems to object here not to the postulation of material abundance but rather to the Populist charge that *people* are responsible for inequality. In this connection it is interesting to note his stress upon "human greed and error" and "human laws." He seems here to ridicule the Populist belief that concrete human activity determines social policies, maintaining either that problems of inequality do not exist, or that neither the social system nor human beings can be held responsible for problems that do exist. Thus, Populist protest becomes necessarily irrational, for it confronts problems that are either nonexistent or inevitable. Even more interesting is the fact that Hofstadter supports this contention with only one Populist publication. This would indicate that he is less concerned at this point with presenting a case for the Populist belief in a "lush natural order" than with establishing a methodological position, his attention being directed not to the first theme itself but to the proposition that conditions are a result of concrete human activity.

He lays the basis for a denial of this proposition by implying that individuals neither created nor bear responsibility for the problems which confronted Populism. This contention takes on crucial significance at a later stage, for it serves as the foundation for the charge that Populists adhered to conspiracy theory: If one believes that individuals are responsible for oppressive conditions, this is regarded as a clear indication of belief in conspiracy theory. Thus, the stress upon utopianism has the effect of discrediting the validity of Populist beliefs, denying the existence of oppressive conditions, and providing a basis for the later charge of conspiracy theory.

Hofstadter states the second theme in the Populist ideology as "the concept of natural harmonies" or "the idea of a natural harmony of interests among the productive classes." Referring specifically to the Populist belief that farmers and workers constituted a class — "there was no fundamental conflict between the farmer and the worker" — this theme applies to the conception of class consciousness, and literally to nothing more. Yet Hofstadter quickly extends its meaning; he contends that belief in the very notion of class necessarily entails an acceptance of conspiracy theory: ". . . predatory behavior existed only because it was initiated and underwritten by a small parasitic minority in the highest places of power." Thus, in the guise of presenting one theme Hofstadter at the same time moves to further contentions: Class consciousness (second theme) leads to the belief that there are only two conflicting classes (third theme), from which it follows that the Populists conceived the opposing class as a small, conspiratorial group (fourth theme). He accomplishes this by treating the three themes together without indicating adequate demarcations, thereby obscuring the fact that each is different and subject to a separate analysis.

In charging that class consciousness necessarily leads to conspiracy theory, Hofstadter can reasonably be viewed as attempting a concerted attack upon the notion of class itself. This, of course, must form a significant portion of his total argument because class and consensus are *antithetical* — to admit the reality of class feeling denies the harmonious character of society.

Yet, can the very notion of class be summarily rejected or taken as a presumption of irrationality simply because it is fashionable in current social theory to do this? This contention raises an even more important problem than simply the validity of the consensus thesis, for if Hofstadter is correct, it follows that conditions giving rise to class feeling were themselves nonexistent. The result is a blanket endorsement of industrial capitalism and a consequent denial that conditions of oppression and concrete economic grievances ever existed.

Hofstadter begins in a clearly condescending tone:

> . . . the Populists adhered, less formally to be sure, but quite persistently, to a kind of social dualism: although they knew perfectly well that society was composed of a number of classes, for all practical purposes only one simple division need be considered. There were two nations.

Yet, by taking only several quotations to support his thesis, Hofstadter contends that Populist thought offered no other critique of the existing society than "The people versus the interests, the public versus the plutocrats, the toiling multitude versus the money power . . . ." It is entirely correct that many Populists did express such sentiments, but Hofstadter's veiled assumption is that the simplicity of these statements insures their invalidity, a judgment made without even trying to ascertain whether these critiques had substance. . . . Hence, by reducing the content of Populist thought to an absurdity, Hofstadter can then conclude by saying:

> The problems that faced the Populists assumed a delusive simplicity: the victory over injustice, the solution for all social ills, was concentrated in the crusade against a single, relatively small but immensely strong interest, the money power.

This "delusive simplicity" was manifested in the Populist stress upon the need for a third party and, when this allegedly failed, in the focus upon a "monolithic solution" — the "money issue." Hofstadter explains the whole significance of the creation of a third party in this manner:

> Since the old political parties were the primary means by which the people were kept wandering in the wilderness, the People's Party advocates insisted, only a new and independent political party could do this essential job.

The tone adopted here is less disturbing than the implicit assumption that there was not a need for the formation of a third party during this period. Can Hofstadter contend that either major party in the decade prior to 1896 was remotely responsive to radicalism, or is he suggesting in effect that the two major parties have always expressed the needs of the society?

On the second point, the concentration upon the "money issue," which also comprises an integral part of his fifth theme, Hofstadter offers only one item in evidence, and even this does not support his point. To illustrate his charge that the Populists believed "there was only one *issue* upon which the money power could really be beaten and this was the money issue," he quotes Bryan's Cross of Gold speech: "When we have restored the money of the Constitution, . . . all other necessary reforms will be possible; but . . . until this is done there is no other reform that can be accomplished." It is clear that Bryan was only saying here that the currency problem must first be solved before other reforms could be carried out, not that it was the only problem, or that its solution guaranteed the solution of other problems. In Bryan's own words once again, "all other necessary reforms will be possible."

Thus, Hofstadter has prejudged the second theme by arguing that the belief in the common ground shared by farmers and workers is patently absurd on its face. Yet he provides no evidence demonstrating its falsity, nor does he even explore areas which could support or deny his contention — the actual activity of farmers and workers themselves. A crucial aspect of Populism is dismissed without jurisdiction in research, the sole reason apparently being that the belief is incompatible with the consensus thesis. If, on the other hand, Hofstadter had discussed Populist grievances from the start and had attributed to these their proper significance, the plausibility of the belief in a farmer-labor coalition could have been at least seriously entertained.[2]

Hofstadter's third theme in Populist ideology — the dualistic version of social struggles — refers to the essential irrationality of the protest, a view the reader is already predisposed to accecpt given the two previous contentions establishing Populism's retrogressive orientation and mythical adherence to a class basis. Here Hofstadter grants that the movement expressed grievances but takes its intensity as presumtpive evidence of irrationality — anything so intense must be *too* intense and, hence, an indication of abnormality. For Hofstadter, "Often, indeed, a deep-lying vein of anxiety showed through. . . ."

Is the notion even entertained that there might be some validity to the Populist charges, or must they constitute prima facie évidence of a "vein of anxity"? It would seem that the historian has acceded to the role of psychoanalyst who can explain authoritatively what the participants *really* meant in their platform, which, of course, is permissible

when it is assumed initially that economic grievances must be unreal. The chief indication of the "vein of anxiety" for the Populists was their belief "that failure of the people to win the final contest peacefully could result only in a total victory for the plutocrats and total extinction of democratic institutions . . . . [Hence] the common fear of an impending apocalypse." This fear had its "most striking articulation" in Ignatius Donnelly's *Caesar's Column*. Although Hofstadter rests his argument in great part upon this book, he biases the reader from the start with the comment,

The convolutions of Donnelly's plot, which includes two tasteless love stories, do little more than entitle the book to be called a novel, and the work is full of a kind of suppressed lasciviousness that one finds often in popular writing of the period.

This interpretation may be seriously challenged, for the book can be viewed more properly as an attempt to point out the seriousness of the economic conflict faced in Donnelly's own day, to plead for government welfare measures, and to show the need for a reaffirmation of ethical values in the face of a narrow technicism accompanying industrialism. These elements can be overlooked easily when the book is regarded merely as "a piece of visionary writing, possibly inspired by the success a few years earlier of [Edward] Bellamy's utopian romance *Looking Backward*." But *Caesar's Column* is not simply a utopian novel. Although utopian aspects make up the negligible portion dealing with technological innovation, the major portion describes conditions which existed at the time when it was written.

Thus, on the seriousness of the conflict, Donnelly had written:

---

[2] A discussion of this nature raises the problem of whether any study of intellectual history can disassociate thought from its embodiment in activity. To divorce the two seriously runs the risk of misunderstanding the thought under consideration, if it does not lead to its outright dismissal from the start. The ultimate test of intellectual history lies in its ability to specify the relationship between thought and action; otherwise, the role of ideas in history serves merely as the plaything of the historian's predilections.

Who is it that is satisfied with the present unhappy condition of society? It is conceded that life is a dark and wretched failure for the great mass of mankind. The many are plundered to enrich the few. Vast combinations depress the price of labor and increase the cost of the necessaries of existence. The rich, as a rule, despise the poor; and the poor are coming to hate the rich. The face of labor grows sullen.

Donnelly's description of labor in the future society further demonstrates that the book is not utopian, for it is no more than an extension of existing conditions: "They seemed to me merely automata, in the hands of some ruthless and unrelenting destiny. They lived and moved, but they were without heart or hope." This conception of the social effects of advanced industrialism anticipated similar statements of the problem by several decades. Emphasizing the importance of government as "the key to the future of the human race," Donnelly suggested that "we have but to expand the powers of government to solve the enigma of the world." *Caesar's Column* may be regarded, then, as a challenge to the beliefs in laissez faire and social Darwinism. "Man separated is man savage; man gregarious is man civilized. A higher development in society requires that this instrumentality of cooperation shall be heightened in its powers." Moreover, the work was concerned with the impact of science upon moral values:

The more they [dominant groups] know of the material world the less they can perceive the spiritual world around and within it. The acquisition of a few facts about nature has closed their eyes to the existence of a God.

Finally, *Caesar's Column* served as a means for suggesting concrete measures applicable to existing conditions. For example, Donnelly called for the abolition of "all interest on money" and of all legislation giving "any man an advantage over any other man; or which tended to concentrate the wealth of the community in the hands of a few." He contended further that limits be imposed "beyond which no man could own property," with the surplus to be invested "under the direction of a governmental board of management, in great works for the benefit of the laboring classes." Other proposals included limits on "the amount of land" to be owned, abolition of "all corporations" or else the turning of "them back into individual partnerships," issuance of "paper money, receivable for all taxes, and secured by the guarantee" of the nation, and creation of an "international paper money" which would be "receivable as legal tender for all debts in all countries."

Hofstadter's fourth theme — the conspiracy theory of history — is based upon the farmers' belief that they were "not simply oppressed but oppressed deliberately." Stemming from the dualistic version of social struggles, deliberate opposition is ascribed by the Populists to the other class. Since the initial conflict is judged irrational, to ascribe hostility to the other side is even more suspect. Thus, Hofstadter presents the notion of conspiracy in this way: The Populists believe that they are deliberately oppressed, which leads to their perception "of the events of their time as the results of a conspiracy."

Once the belief in conspiracy has been established, he rapidly extends the mantle of irrationality around the whole Populist conception of history: "But there is a great difference between locating conspiracies *in* history and saying that history *is*, in effect, a conspiracy . . . ."

Hence, Populists viewed their grievances as a conflict between the "simple virtues and unmitigated villainies of a rural melodrama [that] have been projected on a national and even an international scale." Yet the introduction of conspiracy theory at this point has been made possible only by the prior assumption that conflict is intrinsically irrational.

According to Hofstadter, the conspiracy theory held by the Populists was the belief "that the contraction of currency was a deliberate squeeze," that the bondholders "wanted to be paid not in a common currency but in gold, which was at a premium," and that the moneylenders "wanted as high a premium as possible to be put on their commodity by increasing its scarcity." This aberration seems to have been widespread, for "Wherever one turns in the Populist literature of the nineties one can find this conspiracy theory expressed." As one case in point he examines Mrs. Sarah E. V. Emery's *Seven Financial Conspiracies Which Have Enslaved the American People* (Lansing, Mich., 1888). Once again he introduces the evidence as from a hysterical tract, because it is "dedicated to 'the enslaved people of a dying republic.' "[3] He analyzes the work as "a recital of a series of seven measures passed between 1862 and 1875 which were alleged to be a part of this continuing conspiracy, the total effect of which was to contract the currency of the country further and further," which he lists in a footnote as

. . . the "exception clause" of 1862; the National Bank Act of 1863; the retirement of the greenbacks, beginning in 1866; the "credit-strengthening act" of March 18, 1869; the refunding of the national debt in 1870; the demonetization of silver in 1873; and the destruction of fractional paper currency in 1875.

But does the listing of these seven measures prove that Mrs. Emery was addicted to conspiratorial delusions? In fact, can Hofstadter deny their existence? If not, can he deny that these measures had the effect of contracting the currency? If not, what explanation can he offer for their passage? Did not certain groups support them and stand to gain from their adoption? In short, can Hofstadter seriously contend that legislation is promoted by disinterested groups acting solely in the general interest? It would seem that the consensus thesis requires this position, for he labels as conspiratorial any view maintaining that there *was* a systematic contraction of the currency.

Using the conspiracy theory as an established base line, Hofstadter has prepared the way for his decisive allegation — anti-Semitism was the characteristic expression of Populism. "It was chiefly Populist writers who expressed that identification of the Jew with the usurer and the 'international gold ring' which was the central theme of the American anti-Semitism of the age." This statement is softened somewhat by the reminder that "Populist anti-Semitism was entirely verbal. It was a mode of expression, a rhetorical style, not a tactic or a program. It did not lead to exclusion laws, much less to riots or pogroms." Then, despite his paucity of data, he makes the startling, exaggerated claim, "It is not too much to say that the Greenback-Populist tradi-

[3] There is nothing particularly amusing about Mrs. Emery's dedication. Her father had entreated his children "ever to remember the cause of the oppressed, and ever to condemn a system of legislation calculated to reduce the laboring classes to a state of abject and hopeless servitude; in remembrance of his prophetic words, and his great love for humanity, this little volume is sacredly dedicated to the enslaved people of a dying republic."

tion activated most of what we have of modern popular anti-Semitism in the United States."

The weakness of Hofstadter's case becomes painfully obvious when it is noted that he relies on very few items, some misinterpreted, and on an extremely weak master's thesis. The latter yields two concrete instances of anti-Semitic statements (both by Mrs. Mary Elizabeth Lease), and nothing else whatever that documents Hofstadter's case. Take, for example, his interpretation of a Bryan speech (originally contained in this thesis) in which he suggests that there was such a clear "identification of the silver cause with anti-Semitism" that Bryan was forced "to pause in the midst of his campaign to explain to the Jewish Democrats of Chicago that in denouncing the policies of the Rothschilds he and his silver friends were 'not attacking a race; we are attacking greed and avarice which know no race or religion.'" Yet, when Bryan's speech is placed into context, it appears questionable that he was on the defensive:

[After] Mr. M. Shapiro, on behalf of the Hebrew Democrats presented me a beautiful badge, one of the handsomest received during the campaign . . . . [I said] I appreciate, too, the kindly feeling which has prompted the presentation of this badge by the Hebrew Democrats. Our opponents have sometimes tried to make it appear that we are attacking a race when we denounce the financial policy advocated by the Rothschilds. But we are not; we are as much opposed to the financial policy of J. Pierpont Morgan as we are to the financial policy of the Rothschilds. We are not attacking a race; we are attacking greed and avarice, which know neither race nor religion. I do not know of any class of our people, who by reason of their history, can better sympathize with the struggling masses in this campaign than can the Hebrew race.

Because the Rothschilds are attacked, Hofstadter charges anti-Semitism.

A more valid interpretation might be one that takes into account the sentence immediately preceding the one emphasized. "We are as much opposed to the financial policy of J. Pierpont Morgan as we are to the financial policy of the Rothschilds." Hence, the international banker is the target, whether as a Morgan or a Rothschild, and an extension of the attack upon the latter to the Jewish people is wholly unwarranted. Undoubtedly, there may be instances where reference to the Rothschilds has larger anti-Semitic connotations, but until Hofstadter produces such evidence or demonstrates that the international banker was not a primary concern in its own right, his attack may be regarded, at best, as insightful, though overstated, and, at worst, as an insinuation serving to discredit the Populist movement.

Bryan's final statement — "I do not know of any class of our people, who by reason of their history, can better sympathize with the struggling masses in this campaign than can the Hebrew race" — makes clear that the Populists were themselves aware of the complexity of the problem of anti-Semitism. In fact, it is to their credit that they did not extend this hatred of the Rothschilds to all Jews. This is not surprising, however, when one takes a broader view of Populism, for as John Higham points out, the Populists were the ones "most deeply swayed by the ideals that had made the United States the beloved homeland for thousands of Jews.

Reviewing Hofstadter's case for conspiracy theory, one concludes that it rests primarily on the internal consistency of his themes, not on historical documentation. Using the consensus framework to eliminate the historical and sociological roots of Populism, Hofstadter can then resort to psychological explanations. This raises an extremely important question. What are the implications of psychological analysis for historical methodology?

Basically, psychology imposes a static model of society (in effect, the consensus framework) upon the study of social movements because it requires a standard or reference point by which to judge what is or is not irrational. Thus, all behavior not conforming to the model is categorized as irrational, with the result that the analysis is biased in favor of the status quo and places all protest movements by definition at a disadvantage. However, the fact that radical groups explicitly call for a fundamental change renders them even more susceptible to the charge of irrationality, while conservative groups fare somewhat better in a static model because they can more readily justify themselves in terms of the status quo.

Thus, an obvious defect of psychological analysis is its tendency to highlight deviation from society without directing attention to the causes for the protest. This is precisely the fault of Hofstadter's use of psychology. He conveniently dismisses Populism as an unwarranted protest against nonexisting grievances without admitting into evidence the factors underlying its development. Does this suggest, then, that his charge of conspiracy theory is invalid or that psychological analysis is not relevant for studying history? Since the charge of conspiracy theory can be regarded as suggestive and subject to the ultimate test of documentation, it is wiser not to pass final judgment. However, the manner in which Hofstadter establishes this thesis *is* invalid, exactly the way that psychological analysis is invalid, unless certain limitations are observed. The shortcoming of

conspiracy theory, as in psychology as a whole, is that it should not be used until historical and sociological factors are examined thoroughly. Otherwise, irrational behavior can simply be assumed from the start, when in reality the introduction of factors not apparent on the surface might alter materially the historian's verdict. In short, the historian should use psychology to supplement, not take over, the task of historical research.

Hofstadter's fifth theme — the doctrine of the primacy of money — is treated somewhat later "in connection with the free-silver issue." Referring to the integrity of the Populist leadership, this theme specifically concerns the willingness to support free silver instead of a broader program of reform. Hofstadter characterizes the Populist leadership as "a ragged elite of professional men, rural editors, third-party veterans, and professional reformers," who "had been subsisting for long years upon a monotonous diet of failure." They turned to free silver because they "hungered for success as major-party leaders knew it, and this left them open to temptation: they could, without too much difficulty, be persuaded to give up a large part of their program if they felt that this was the way to win." Since their movement was continually beset with a "lack of funds," "out of necessity, and not out of corruption," it was "for sale cheap," and "found its takers in the silver interest." The implications are clear: The Populist leaders succumbed to the silver interests because gaining office was more important to them than standing for fundamental reforms. Hence, they were not basically radical. . . .

The charge of Populist opportunism is a particularly fitting culmination for Hofstadter's analysis because it insures against any examination either of Populist grievances or the specific measures designed to correct the situation. Moreover, his treatment of Populist leadership reveals several deficiencies which can be said to characterize the analysis as a whole. First, he demonstrates a naive assumption that radicalism could always find expression within the two-party system, that no structural difficulties existed to the rational voicing of discontent, in short, that the American political system has always been responsive to the needs of oppressed groups. The implication in this fifth theme, then, is: The Populists had no objective reason for supporting Bryan, so that the very fact of their attempt at fusion is presumptive evidence that they were not radical or not sincere.

Second, and related to this, Hofstadter ignores the historical development of the protest under consideration; that is, the fact these men long supported specific remedies for a progressively worsening situation is apparently not an important factor in their decision. Instead, he grossly oversimplifies the issue of fusion by failing to bring out the dilemma confronting the Populists and the painfulness of their choice. Rather than indicate that the problem had been discussed for several years in the local Populist press and in the correspondence of Populist leaders, he simply charges a colossal sellout on the part of a few leaders. Undoubtedly, there are grounds for questioning the wisdom of fusion, as did Lloyd and Donnelly, and for pointing to the possibly devious actions of some leaders, for example, Taubeneck, but this still overlooks the larger problem: Could the Populists actually have pursued any other course? Did not they stand for measures other than free silver, and did not they have a radical influence upon the Democratic party? Hence, did fu-

sion as it developed on a larger scale signify only that the Populists never really committed themselves to a radical position?

Hofstadter's preoccupation with present values is reflected most clearly in his attempt to justify the consensus thesis, for he intersperses throughout the discussion a systematic construction of the typical representative of Populism — the capitalist-on-the-make. Since protest *qua* protest cannot be admitted, he very carefully proceeds to create an ideal farmer-type who conforms remarkably to the values of present-day America and, hence, appears not unreasonable to the reader. He finds this rank-and-file Populist to be simply "inspired to make money," so that his protest, while highly irrational because conditions do not warrant it, is still only directed to securing a larger share of the pie. It is essential to note the emergence of this image, which William Appleman Williams correctly calls an attempt to "restructure reality according to the model."

In chapter one, page one, the farmer-image is presented as unquestioned fact: "The farmer himself, in most cases, was in fact inspired to make money, and such self-sufficiency as he actually had was usually forced upon him by a lack of transportation or markets, or by the necessity to save cash to expand his operations." The key words "inspired to make money" and "to expand his operations" plant the image and define *in advance* the nature of Populist protest — the need for "status." But in employing the concept of a status revolution Hofstadter offers no documentation, but relies instead on the device of repetition:

Rank in society! That was close to the heart of the matter, for the farmer was beginning to realize acutely not merely that the best of the world's goods were to be had in the cities and that the urban middle and upper classes had much more of them than he did but also that he was losing status and respect as compared with them.

Using "rank in society" as the defining characteristic of Populist protest, Hofstadter moves step-by-step in this image-building process to the conclusion that the farmer was in reality only "a harrassed little country businessman." How radical, then, can the protest be of "a harrassed little country businessman" who made more money "on the process of appreciation than on the sale of crops," who lived in a society attached "not to the land but to land values," who regarded fresh lands as "a risk valve," and whose life was characterized as "so speculative, so mobile, so mechanized, so 'progressive,' so thoroughly imbued with the commercial spirit"?

In presenting this critique it was necessary to confine the remarks to Hofstadter's own evidence and in that way raise questions concerning the validity of his scholarship. It is suggested, however, that a re-searching of Populist manuscripts and newspaper shows even more effectively the weaknesses of his interpretation, for the evidence on each of his themes points to an entirely different conclusion. For example, the Populists were far from adopting a retrogressively utopian view towards society; many of them accepted the fact of industrialism and sought to democratize its impact through highly specific measures. They did not hold to outdated producers' values but reasoned that farmers and workers were being placed in precisely the same economic position vis-à-vis the total society; hence, actual attempts at coalition between the two groups were made. Tens of thousands of Populist statements show that anti-Semitism was so infrequently mentioned that it might be contended that there was less, not more, anti-Semitism in the movement than in the rest of society. Finally, the issue of fusion was so complex and rooted so firmly in the difficulties of making protest heard during this period that the charge of a Populist betrayal of principles is not warranted.

In the last analysis, however, this critique is directed to Hofstadter's methodological assumptions because in less capable hands than his own such procedures can only lead to the denial that protest ever existed in American society. Radicalism then becomes wholly discredited as a rational alternative while the present-day society is uncritically accepted. If it were Hofstadter's intention, on the other hand, to write a suggestive essay designed to stimulate discussion, then he has achieved his purpose.

Walter T. K. Nugent: KANSAS POPULISM: A CASE STUDY

Although both Walter Nugent and Norman Pollack reject the revisionist view of Populism, Nugent's study attacks revisionism on different grounds. In the concluding chapter of his book the author summarizes his findings on Kansas Populism. While he is cautious about generalizing beyond the scope of his study, it is clear that Nugent believes that his work undermines important revisionist contentions.

THE FOREGOING chapters have narrated the story of the Populist movement in Kansas, with special reference to the relations between the Populists and non-American ideas, groups, and persons. Although a sizable body of literature appeared during the 1950's that asserted that the Populists were deeply hostile to things non-American, the Kansas story does not support those assertions. In fact, it supports something more like the opposite of each of the outstanding points of criticism.

The Populists have been accused of nativism, both of a personal kind and of an ideological kind; instead, they were friendlier and more receptive to foreign persons and foreign institutions than the average of their contemporary political opponents. They have been accused of "conspiracy-mindedness"; for them, however, tangible fact quite eclipsed neurotic fiction. They have been accused of anti-Semitism, both personal and ideological; instead they consistently got along well with their Jewish neighbors and consistently refrained from extending their dislike of certain financiers, who happened to be Jews, to Jews in general. They have been accused of chauvinism and jingoism, especially with reference to the Spanish-American War; instead, such lukewarm support as they gave collec-

tively to Cuban intervention was based on quite different grounds, and as a group they strongly opposed the imperialism that the war engendered. Finally, they have been accused of selling out their vaunted reform principles by seeking political fusion with the Democratic party, especially in 1896, and thus of revealing a neurotic instability; but instead, fusion was for them a legitimate means to the accomplishment of real, if limited, reform. In the case of Kansas, the largest of the wheat-belt Populist states, the five principal criticisms of Populism voiced by recent writers not only do not square with the facts, but should be replaced with a viewpoint so much in contrast as to be practically the opposite. Briefly put, this viewpoint is as follows.

Populism in Kansas was a political response to economic distress. From the early days of the Farmers' Alliance, the progenitor of the People's party, to about 1892, relief of economic difficulty was virtually the sole reason for the party's existence; after 1892 this purpose was alloyed to some degree with the desire of the party to perpetuate itself as a political organism. In both periods, however, economic difficulties remained the party's chief reason for being, and relief of them its main objective. Populism

Reprinted from *The Tolerant Populists: Kansas Populism and Nativism* by Walter T. K. Nugent, pp. 231–243, by permission of The University of Chicago Press.

called for the enactment of a set of legislative reforms by state and federal gov-
ernments and accepted the extension of
governmental power involved in such enactment. In its most complete and ideal
form, the Populist program appeared in
the national party platform of 1892, the
Omaha Platform," but this platform bore
no more nor less relation to the practical
operations of the party than platforms
usually do. In Kansas the People's party
placed its emphasis consistently on the
three questions of land, money, and
transportation, which were the issues
causing greatest distress in that particular state. Since monetary reform seemed
to have the broadest political appeal of
all the reforms called for in the Populist
program, it received more stress than the
rest of the program at the time (1894–97)
when the party seemed to have its best
chance of succeeding.

As Populism followed the ways of practical party politics in the program that
it offered and in the issues it chose to
stress, it took a practical approach to its
sources of support as well. Economic
distress cut across lines of religion, of
nationality origins, of race, of previous
political affiliation, even of occupation
and of wealth and status. To so great an
extent was this the case that it is not even
accurate to say that the Populists accepted or sought the support of third-
party men, Republicans, Democrats, immigrants of many kinds, organized labor,
city dwellers, and others, to broaden
their agriculturalist base. For these
groups were in and of Populism from the
beginning. The job of the party leaders
was therefore not so much to attract new
groups but to be sure that the party
program appealed to each of those
groups already there and to spread the
Populist message to further individual
members of the existing coalition, of

which the lowest common denominator
was a desire for one or more specific economic reforms.

As a result, large numbers of every
politically consequential foreign-born
group then in Kansas, with the exception
of the Mennonites, became active Populists. Party leaders received this support
warmly and eagerly, except for one or
two occasions: the 1894 state convention
and probably the one of 1890. At those
times, certain influential leaders supported the non-economic issues of
women's suffrage and prohibition so vo-
cally that they led the party to take positions unacceptable to many foreign-born
groups. Even here, however, the attitude
of these leaders to the foreign-born was
one of indifference not of hostility. The
fact of the matter seems to be, to judge
by statements made by the delegates on
the floor of the 1894 convention, that
many Populists were simply unconcerned
with ethnic groups or foreign matters;
they were neither favorable nor hostile,
except when they thought they might
justifiably appeal to ethnic bloc votes or
when they cited examples of enlightened
foreign institutions to document their
own reform program. To the great majority of Populists, in 1894 and at other
times, foreignness and certainly Jewish-
ness were simply not affective categories.
For practical political reasons, among
others, the Populists expressed themselves favorably toward foreign groups,
either abroad or close at hand. This was
certainly true of the fusionists; it was
true of the non-fusionists except when
women's suffrage and prohibition got in
the way; it was even true, at times, of
the Middle-of-the-Road group, which
combined an antibanker (including English, Anglo-Jewish, and Wall Street
banker) rhetoric with some benevolence
toward immigrants as individuals.

Many leading Populists were in fact first or second generation immigrants. In the 1890's the Populists surpassed the Republicans in the proportion of their state legislators who were foreign-born. Foreign-born Populists abounded among county-level officeholders, county committeemen, precinct workers, and delegates to county, district, and state political conventions. Wherever an ethnic group existed, there existed as well its Populist voters and Populist leaders, with the exception of the Mennonites, who were undeviatingly Republican. The Populists, however, had immigrant blocs of their own, especially on the frequent occasions of county and state-level fusion with the Democrats. The party organization appealed to foreign-language groups with pamphlets, newspapers, and campaign speakers. They presented much the same arguments to their polyglot audience as the party was making to the English-speaking voters. The only difference was in window dressing, such as testimonials from Prince Bismarck and from German political economists in support of silver coinage. At their 1894 state convention, and prior and subsequently in their newspapers, the Populists forthrightly condemned the American Protective Association, the most influential and widespread nativist organization since the Know-Nothings.

On three contemporaneous issues relating directly to immigrants, the Populists took positions that might seem at first glance to have been nativistic, but in each case their attitude to the immigrant was neutral or favorable. When they attacked "alien" landholding, they were attacking landlordism, not the immigrant small landholder. When they called for an end to contract or "pauper labor" immigration, they clearly excepted "worthwhile" or "sturdy" immigrants and based their position on labor competition, not on racism. When their congressmen supported the Lodge-McCall literacy test to restrict immigration, they apparently did so as the only practical way to enact the bill's riders, which would have lessened labor competition, and almost never expressed approval of the philosophy of superior and inferior, desirable or undesirable, races put forward by Lodge and the Immigration Restriction League. In each of these three instances the Populists based their actions on reasonable economic grounds, if not especially perceptive or laudable ones. Their aim was to attract the political support of organized labor, of tenant farmers, and very likely of Irish-Americans.

The rhetoric of Populism was highly charged with nationalism, but it was a nineteenth-century kind of nationalism that did not include the nativistic or anti-Semitic characteristics of some twentieth-century right-wing nationalists. Only two foreign groups fell under the censure of any considerable number of Populists. This censure was a consequence of two issues firmly rooted in economic realities and in neither case did they grow out of or were they extended to racial or nativistic antagonism. The two groups were English or Anglo-Jewish financiers and English or Anglo-Irish landlords, respectively responsible in part for money stringency and for large landholding. Many Populists feared that the trend toward tighter money and tighter land would continue unchecked unless these two groups, *and their American or Gentile associates*, were stopped. In both cases the antipathy of the Populists clearly extended to all malevolent financiers, monopolists, and land barons, whether English or American, whether Jew or Gentile, whether native or alien. For the

Populists, or many of them, to have laid their troubles at the door of a mixed group of English, Anglo-Jewish, and American capitalists may have been naïve and simplistic, but the point is that the common denominator of their hostility was not nativism or anti-Semitism but distrust and dislike of a truly unsympathetic economic class. In some cases their anti-English attitude transcended this economic base, since the economic problem meshed so well with the rather widespread anti-English attitude shared by many nineteenth-century Americans as part of the American Revolutionary tradition. But the English people escaped the censure placed upon certain financially powerful Englishmen, and Jewish financiers escaped any blame whatever as Jews, although a few of them, as investment bankers, shared the criticisms heaped by the Populists, or rather, some of their more outspoken rhetoricians, upon the wickedness of powerful financial interests in general. This was certainly the case with the terms "Shylock" and "Rothschild," which appeared with some frequency in Populist literature but which were cachets not of Jewish conspiracy but of oppressive finance.

So far did Populist expressions of friendliness to Jews as individuals, in Kansas and elsewhere, to Jews as a group, to English immigrants, to English institutions such as co-operatives and public ownership of utilities, outweigh the expressions that might be construed with effort as Anglophobic or anti-Semitic, and so specious are the grounds upon which the Populists have been accused of Anglophobia, anti-Semitism, or nativism, that these accusations must simply fall without support. There is an exception that proves the rule. A handful of Populists sometimes let their an-

tipathies include "racial characteristics" of these two groups, especially the English, and thereby they evidenced irrationality and prejudice. They were atypical. Many, in fact nearly all, of these Populists were attached to the Middle-of-the-Road Populist splinter group in 1894 and 1896. This group attempted to overthrow the recognized state leadership, whose reform credentials were at least as old and respectable as the dissidents'; it was in all probability subsidized by the Republican state organization; and it received the support of less than 1 per cent of the rank and file at the polls in 1896 and of the Populist press.

In what, then, did their nationalism consist? It is difficult to answer such a question, because to accuse such a pragmatic, anti-intellectual people as these agrarians of having possessed "concepts" or "ideas," much more a "system," is itself a distortion. They did, however, possess felt attitudes that were forced into words to form the rhetoric of their speeches and editorials. Needless to say, the scribes and leaders of Populism came closer than anyone else to expressing these views in logical form, subject, of course, to political exigencies. But it can be assumed that their rhetoric must have been congenial to the rank and file — otherwise they would have been unable to attract and to hold that rank and file. Nonetheless, the rhetoric is undoubtedly more radical, more logically organized, and much more explicit than the views of the mass of the party. In their rhetoric, Populist nationalism consisted of a feeling that the United States was a different *kind* of political society from any that had ever existed before and therefore more worth preserving than any previous one. America was not just another nation-state but an embodiment of certain ideals. It was the embodiment of democratic republicanism: a society where the people rule, where the governed consent to their governors, where the rights of life, liberty, and property are protected because this very protection is the object of their own self-government. It was the embodiment, too, of economic democracy: where resources wanted only honest labor to be translated into the reality of abundance, where opportunity was equal, where the distribution of the nation's wealth was equitable. It was the antithesis of Europe and Europe's corruption, decadence, parasitical upper classes, stagnation, and economic and political oppression. It was a place, in short, where the people rule for themselves and for the protection of their natural rights. Or, at least, so it should have been.

Yet who were the people? The answer is already implied. The people were those who believed in the ideals of democratic republicanism, of economic democracy, and of freedom from European conditions of life. The people were those who actively sought the preservation of those ideals. They were those who labored by their own hands, who had equal opportunities to labor and to accumulate, who used the resources of the United States to produce their own and the nation's wealth. They were those who created wealth rather than those who manipulated wealth already produced. Very often this legitimate wealth-producing activity was defined by the Populists as agricultural and laboring activity; those who farmed or labored were by definition the real people. This corresponded conveniently both to what might roughly be called the Jeffersonian-Jacksonian tradition and to the actual political bases of the People's party's support. Translated into the rhetoric of a political campaign, it often meant emphasizing "the producing classes" or the common bonds of "the farming and laboring people."

The conscious derivation for all of this was the American Revolution, and secondarily, the War of 1812. These struggles successfully created a nation embodying this set of ideals. Such conscious roots made it easy, of course, for some Populists to look upon the machinations of English financiers as a third and final attempt by England to subjugate America. It was primarily through the American Revolution that a nation of, by, and for the people was created and through it that all that was wrong with Europe and Britain was left behind.

Consequently, it was up to the people — often implying the farmers and laborers—to see to it that this nation, this unique society, did not perish from the earth. Who threatened its extinction? Certainly not the refugee from European misery, at least so long as he, too, believed in American republicanism and opportunity. In this unique kind of nation the doors were open to those who wished legitimately to share its benefits. The goods of this nation were not to be shut up inside for the exclusive use of those already there but rather to beckon as to a flourishing haven those who wished to escape the oppression of a decadent Europe. The nation was, in Lincoln's words, a last, best hope of earth. The immigrant was to show his good faith in these ideals by becoming a citizen and remaining permanently (as the Populist's alien land law provided) and by not attempting to destroy the opportunity of individuals already possessing it (as Populist demands for an end to "pauper labor" immigration showed). For an immigrant to take away the job of an

American laborer was unnecessary any-
way, since opportunity and America were
virtually synonymous.

The "worthwhile" or "sturdy" immigrant was not, then, the enemy of American nationality. In fact, he seemed to
justify the Populist approach to American nationality — certainly he did in the
case of immigration agricultural colonies
in Kansas, which had been very successful — and he was therefore quite wel-
come. But who then *was* the enemy? To
most Populists who thought about the
matter beyond their immediate economic
distress — and by no means all of them
thought through their views of American
nationalism with anything like the com-
pleteness that this sketch might imply —
the enemy lay in certain recently emer-
gent opportunities for malevolence.
America was shifting from a predominantly rural and agricultural nation to
one predominantly urban and industrial.
This shift was in no way evil in itself.
Populist spokesmen such as Senators
Peffer and Harris had expressly denied
any hope of turning back the clock, and
if they were not absolutely delighted
with a process that seemed to be top-
pling the farmers and their allies from
political and economic predominance (if
indeed they had ever possessed it), they
were determined to live with such a
trend. What is more, they were determined to see that these changes should
benefit all the people and not just a few;
that they should take place in such ways
as to guarantee democratic republicanism and economic democracy. The majority of them therefore accepted indus-
trialization but condemned monopoly,
accepted banking and finance but condemned usury and financial sleight of
hand, welcomed accumulation but condemned economic feudalism, welcomed

enterprise but condemned speculation.
It was not industry and urbanism that
oppressed them, they thought, but their
abuse.

For most Populists these considerations
identified the enemy well enough. An
appealing program, aimed conveniently
at the relief of immediate distress as well
as at the placing of new trends within
the old ideals, could be constructed without further ado. A rhetoric quickly
emerged that concerned itself with attacking landlordism, transportation monopoly, and money shortages, and this
rhetoric remained the basic vehicle of
Populist ideas from start to finish. In a
minority of cases, however, it seemed
convenient to personalize the enemy, and
in doing so, some Populists passed the
bounds of precise statement. At times,
American financiers and monopolists
such as the Belmonts, Morgans, and Van-
derbilts, English financiers such as the
Rothschilds, American and English land
and mortgage loan companies, and prominent American statesmen such as Sherman, McKinley, and Cleveland, together
seemed to form a common and inimical
class dedicated to the people's overthrow. Ever since the Civil War this
group seemed to have conspired to bring
about the economic destruction of the
farmers and their allies. This minority
of Populists thereby dealt with the
money question in terms of a "money
power." Yet even they nearly all used
the term "conspiracy" in a general sense
to mean the common attitudes of an en-
trenched and powerful minority, and
only a tiny proportion meant by the term
an explicit conspiratorial agreement, as
when they referred to Ernest Seyd and
the "Hazzard Circular" of the sixties and
seventies. But most Populists did not
voice this line, a fact more remarkable

if one grants that rhetoric tends to be more radical than the general feeling of its political following. This "conspiracy" was, in addition, a financial one and not a Jewish or English one. To look at a close-knit community of interest and to see in the mind's eye a conspiracy is not necessarily great irrationality but rather a lack of factual knowledge about the competitive methods of late nineteenth-century capitalism. If antibanker, anti-monopoly, or anticapitalist statements formed fairly frequent themes in Populist rhetoric, Populists of every hue made it clear that it was usury, irresponsible economic power, and minority rule that they were opposing and not the industrial revolution, urbanism, or capitalism and banking as such. The abuse of new trends, not the trends themselves, had driven them, they felt, from their once uncontested eminence. Now they wanted to regain that eminence and accepted the fact that it could never again be theirs alone. If agrarian class predominance was over and done with, plutocratic class predominance should be scuttled before it progressed any further. Then economic democracy would be reborn.

The Populist view of American nationality, with its stress on democratic republicanism and economic democracy, was therefore intended to be at once majoritarian, individualistic, and humanitarian. That it was a nationalism naïvely humanitarian rather than aggressive appeared very clearly in the Populists' approach to the Cuban insurrection and the Spanish-American War. They sympathized deeply with the insurgent Cubans and viewed their uprising as a struggle for freedom and democracy much like the American uprising of the 1770's. In Kansas this sympathy expressed itself in a moral support for the insurrectionists that sprang

from a confident view of their own moral righteousness. Nonetheless, the Populist press and Populist congressmen held back from armed intervention, took a cautious attitude to the blowing up of the *Maine*, restrained themselves from anything more vigorous than sympathetic gestures toward the Cubans in spite of the Spanish "despotism" and "Weylerism" they believed the Cubans to be suffering, and in unison with their Democratic neighbors hoped that war could be avoided. This was very close to the Republic position also. When war came, they supported it as everyone else did, but until then their humanitarian sympathy for the Cubans was checked by the fear that a war beginning with Cuban intervention could only benefit large financial interests. The Kansas Republicans' coolness toward Cuban intervention resulted mainly from the caution that McKinley maintained into April, 1898, and the desire of the Kansas Republicans to support their own administration. The Populists avoided the Republicans' scornful references to Cuban or Spanish racial inferiority and far more frequently than the Republicans took a humanitarian view of the matter. In Kansas the Populists were not violent jingoes. Furthermore, unlike the Republicans in their area, and other people elsewhere, the official Populist position on the question of American imperial expansion for commercial or military purposes, which arose after Dewey's victory in Manila Bay, was to join the Democrats in opposing expansion and in demanding that the United States leave the Philippines and other potential colonies alone. They were interested in the spread of American democratic ideals, in the overthrow of Spanish oppression of Cuba, if this could be done without the commitment of American armed forces, but not at all in American conquest or colonization. Populism in Kansas apparently lost many adherents because of this stand, but it remained the official party position nevertheless.

It is worth noting that Populist opposition to imperialism was much more firmly expressed than Populist sympathy to the Cuban insurrectionists, because the Democratic party was also much less firm on the latter question than on the former. As a matter of fact, official Populist rhetoric was tailored to fit the political exigencies involved in getting along with the Democrats not only on the war and imperalism issues but on most other questions as well. Political fusion with the Democrats on all levels marked Kansas Populism very strongly, and to some writers, fusion has meant that the Populists lacked any real dedication to the principles they so vigorously espoused. But the Populist movement chose political means to accomplish its program of economic reform; it was a political party, not a pressure group or an ideological front; for better or worse it therefore bound itself to use partisan methods. If one looks no further than the Omaha platform of 1892 to find out what Populism stood for and then observes that many planks in that platform were soft-pedaled in 1892 and later for the sake of fusion and political success, one might assume that Populist devotion to reform principles was a sham. But this is a superficial view. Fusion was the only apparent way to achieve any reforms, any accomplishment of any principles at all, and the degree to which the People's party was willing to fuse with the Democrats in Kansas was the degree to which it possessed political common sense. The identification of fusion with dedication to principle, rather than with a sellout, comes into even greater relief as soon as

one recalls the shabby story of the Middle-of-the-Road Populists, those self-styled simon-pure reformers who almost certainly connived at the defeat of the reform party with the local Republican organization. The prevalence of fusion sentiment indicates as well the willingness of the Populists to seek out and accept the support of the foreign-born blocs that ordinarily made their political home in the Democratic party. It also indicates their pragmatic approach to political action, their willingness to use an obvious means at hand to achieve legitimate political ends, and their flexibility, which stood in such contrast to the rigidity of the Middle-of-the-Road Populists.

The political horse sense that provided them with their receptivity to fusion was a natural outgrowth of the immediacy of the distress from which their movement sprang. It accounted, too, for the apparent anomaly of a radical program based on conservative ideals. For the Populists of Kansas were not a collection of rag-tag calamity howlers, ne'er-do-wells, and third-party malcontents, as William Allen White and others have suggested, but a large body of people of diverse occupational, wealth-holding, and status levels. As a group they were hardly distinguishable from their Republican neighbors, except for a probably higher mortgage indebtedness, and their greater degree of political and economic awareness. The great majority could be called "middle class," and they were interested in preserving what they considered to be their middle-class American ideals and substance. These were being threatened, they felt, not by the facts of industrialism and urbanism but by their existing *shape*. To change that shape, they settled upon the device of a political party.

Their view of the future was one in

which many wrongs would have to be righted, many present trends would have to be redirected to conform to old ideals, for that future to become acceptable. Yet they were confident that this would happen. In several ways they were confused, ill-informed, and behind the times. They were unaware of urban problems, for example, and they never understood that money reform was basically a solution only to agricultural problems, if indeed to them, and not a solution for growing monopoly or for inequities of wealth distribution. Yet if this is true, it is true as well to acquit them of nativism, anti-Semitism, conspiracy-mindedness, jingoism, lack of principle, and of living in some neurotic agrarian dream world. They were bound together not by common neuroses but by common indebtedness, common price squeezes, common democratic and humanitarian ideals, and common wrath at the infringement of them. From this wrath rose the Farmers' Alliance, and from the Alliance their ultimate instrument of protest, the People's party. The Populists were far too concerned with land, money, and transportation, and also, later on, with the mechanics of winning and keeping public office, to have much time to worry about whether their ideals were mythical or their anxieties neurotic. Tight money and foreclosure sales were the products of nobody's imagination. Even in their rhetoric they were too busy preaching positive reforms in a depression to be concerned with racism or anti-Semitism or agrarian Arcadias; and in their practical political activities, they took all the help they could get.

The Populists were liberal nationalists bringing to radical social changes a radical response. By such means they meant to re-assert what they considered to be the fundamental ideals upon which their society had previously depended — in their view of history — and must continue to depend — in their view of political philosophy. They undertook this task in the Kansas of the 1890's, with its particular kind of social structure, its particular distribution of wealth and income, its specific economic conditions, and its peculiar laws and traditions. These particularities form the limits of historical analogy, and they give no grounds for making the Populists the gawky ancestors of Father Coughlin or of Senator Joseph R. McCarthy. They make it very difficult to call the Populists the descendants of the Jeffersonians and Jacksonians or the precursors of Progressivism or the New Deal, although with these movements the Populists shared a considerable body of ideals. They make it unrealistic even to equate the Kansas Populists with Populists of other regions or other states.

This particular set of facts, however, allows the Populists of Kansas to be judged on their own grounds. The verdict is very simple. They were people who were seeking the solution of concrete economic distress through the instrumentality of a political party. By this means they would not only help themselves but they would redirect, not reverse, the unsatisfactory trends of their time to correspond with the ideals of the past. This involved profoundly the political co-operation of the foreign-born, and it involved a deep respect and receptivity for non-American institutions and ideas.

C. Vann Woodward: POPULISM AND THE INTELLECTUALS

C. Vann Woodward, an historian of the South and biographer of the Southern Populist leader, Tom Watson, also has many reservations about revisionist appraisals. While more willing than many critics to accept the insights of Hofstadter, Woodward believes that the revisionist image of Populism is seriously distorted; in his essay he attempts to explain how this hostile interpretation gained wide acceptance among intellectuals in the 1940's and 1950's.

D URING the long era of the New Deal, one had little difficulty living in comparative congeniality with the Populist heritage. The two periods had much in common, and it was easy to exaggerate the similarities and natural to seek antecedents and analogies in the earlier era. Because of the common setting of severe depression and economic dislocation, Populism seemed even closer to the New Deal than did Progressivism, which had a setting of prosperity. Common to both Populists and New Dealers was an antagonism to the values and dominant leaders of the business community. Among both was a sense of urgency and an edge of desperation about the demand for reform. And in both, so far as the South and West were concerned, agricultural problems were the most desperate, and agrarian reforms occupied the center of attention. It seemed entirely fitting that Hugo Black of Alabama and Harry Truman of Missouri — politicians whose political style and heritage were strongly Populistic — should lead New Deal reform battles. From many points of view the New Deal was neo-Populism. . . .

Many intellectuals made themselves at home in the neo-Populist coalition and embraced the Populist heritage. They had prepared the way for the affiliation in the twenties when they broke with the genteel tradition, adopted the mucker pose, and decided that conventional politics and the two major parties were the province of the boobocracy and professional politicians were clowns or hypocrites. In the thirties intellectuals made naïve identification with farmers and workers and supported their spokesmen with enthusiasm. The Populist affinity outlasted the New Deal, survived the war, and perhaps found its fullest expression in the spirit of indulgent affection with which intellectuals often supported Harry Truman and his administration.

Even before Truman left the White House, however, the Populist identification fell into disgrace, and intellectuals began to repudiate the heritage. "Populist" suddenly became a term of opprobrium, in some circles a pejorative epithet. This resulted from no transfer of affection to Truman's successor, for there was very little of that among intellectuals. The origins of the altered temper came earlier.

Disenchantment of the intellectual with the masses was well under way in the forties. Mass support for evil causes in Germany and elsewhere helped to undermine the faith. The liberal's feelings of

From C. Vann Woodward, "The Populist Heritage and the Intellectual," *The Burden of Southern History* (Baton Rouge, 1960), pp. 141–166. Reprinted by permission of the author.

guilt and impotence were reflected in the interest that the writings of Sören Kierkegaard and Reinhold Niebuhr aroused, and the mood of self-flagellation was expressed in the vogue of the novels of Franz Kafka and George Orwell. The shock of the encounter with McCarthyism sustained and intensified the mood. Liberals and intellectuals bore the brunt of the McCarthyite assault on standards of decency. They were rightly alarmed and felt themselves betrayed. They were the victims of a perversion of the democracy they cherished, a seamy and sinister side of democracy to which they now guiltily realized they had too often turned a blind or indulgent eye. Stung by consciousness of their own naïveté, they responded with a healthy impulse to make up for lost time and confront their problem with all the critical resources at their command. The consequence has been a formidable and often valuable corpus of social criticism.

Not one of the critics, not even the most conservative, is prepared to repudiate democracy. There is general agreement that the fault lay in some abuse or perversion of democracy and was not inherent in democracy itself. All the critics are aware that these abuses and perversions had historic antecedents and had appeared in various guises and with disturbing frequency in national history. These unhappy tendencies are variously described as "mobism," "direct democracy," or "plebecitarianism," but there is a surprising and apparently spontaneous consensus of preference for "Populism." Although the word is usually capitalized, the critics do not as a rule limit its reference to the political party that gave currency to the term. While there is general agreement that the essential characteristics designated by the term are best illustrated by an agrarian move-

ment in the last decade of the nineteenth century, some of the critics take the liberty of applying it to movements as early as the Jacksonians, or earlier, and to twentieth-century phenomena as well.

Reasons for this convergence from several angles upon "Populism" as the appropriate designation for an abhorred abuse are not all clear. A few, however, suggest themselves. Populism is popularly thought of as an entirely Western affair, Wisconsin as a seedbed of the movement, and old Bob La Follette as a foremost exponent. None of these assumptions is historically warranted, but it is true that Senator McCarthy came from Wisconsin, that much of his support came from the Middle West, and that there are some similarities between the two movements. The impression of similarity has been enhanced by the historical echo of their own alarm that modern intellectuals have caught in the rather hysterical fright with which Eastern conservatives reacted to Populism in the nineties.

This essay is not concerned with the validity of recent analysis of the "radical right" and its fascistic manifestations in America. It is concerned only with the tendency to identify Populism with these movements and with the implied rejection of the Populist tradition.

* * *

For the dubious distinction of being the leading Populist section, the South is in fact a strong contender; if the test used be merely quasi-Populism the preeminence of the former Confederacy is unchallengeable. It was easily the most solidly Bryan section of the country, and its dogged loyalty long outlasted that of the Nebraskan's native state. However, a more important test was third-party Populism, the genuine article. The remarkable strength the Populists manifested in the Lower South was gained against far more formidable obstacles than any ever encountered in the West. For there they daily faced the implacable dogmas of racism, white solidarity, white supremacy, and the bloody shirt. There was indeed plenty of "thought control and racist bigotry and lynch-spirit," but the Populists were far more often the victims than the perpetrators. They had to contend regularly with foreclosure of mortgages, discharge from jobs, eviction as tenants, exclusion from church, withholding of credit, boycott, social ostracism, and the endlessly reiterated charge of racial disloyalty and sectional disloyalty. Suspicion of loyalty was in fact *the* major psychological problem of the Southern Populists, as much so perhaps as the problem of loyalty faced by radicals of today. They contended also against cynical use of fraud comparable with any used against Reconstruction, methods that included stuffed ballot boxes, packed courts, stacked registration and election boards, and open bribery. They saw election after election stolen from them and heard their opponents boast of the theft. They were victims of mobs and lynchers. Some fifteen Negroes and several white men were killed in the Georgia Populist campaign of 1892, and it was rare that a major election in the Lower South came off without casualties.

Having waged their revolt at such great cost, the Southern Populists were far less willing to compromise their principles than were their Western brethren. It was the Western Populists who planned and led the movement to sell out the party to the Silverites, and the Southern Populists who fought and resisted the drift to quasi-Populism. The Southerners were consistently more radical, more insistent upon their economic reforms, and more stubbornly unwilling to lose their party identity in the watered-down quasi-Populism of Bryan than were the Westerners. . . .

In their analysis of the radical right of modern America, the new critics have made use of the concept of "status resentment" as the political motivation of their subjects. They distinguish between "class politics," which has to do with the correction of economic deprivations, and "status politics," which has no definite solutions and no clear-cut legislative program but responds to irrational appeals and vents aggression and resentment for status insecurity upon scapegoats — usually ethnic minorities. Seymour Martin Lipset, who appears at times to include Populism in the category, has outlined the conditions typical of periods when status politics become ascendant. These are, he writes, "periods of prosperity, especially when full employment is accompanied by inflation, and when many individuals are able to improve their economic position." But the conditions under which Populism rose were exactly the opposite: severe depression, critical unemployment, and crippling currency contraction, when few were able to improve their economic position — and certainly not farmers in a cash-crop staple agriculture.

The Populist may have been bitten by status anxieties, but if so, they were certainly not bred of upward social mobility, and probably few by downward mobility either — for the simple reason that there was not much further downward for most Populists to go, and had not been for some time. Populism was hardly "status politics," and I should hesitate to call it "class politics." It was more nearly "interest politics," and more specifically "agricultural interest politics." Whatever concern the farmers might have had for their status was overwhelmed by desperate and immediate economic anxieties. Not only their anxieties but their proposed solutions and remedies were economic. While their legislative program may have often been naïve and inadequate, it was almost obsessively economic and, as political platforms go, little more irrational than the run-of-the-mill.

Yet one of the most serious charges leveled against the Populists in the reassessment of the new critics is an addiction to just the sort of irrational obsession that is typical of status politics. This is the charge of anti-Semitism. . . .

In the voluminous literature of the nineties on currency and monetary problems — problems that were much more stressed by silverites and quasi-Populists than by radical Populists — three symbols were repetitively used for the plutocratic adversary. One was institutional, "Wall Street," and two were ethnic, the British and Jewish bankers. Wall Street was by far the most popular and has remained so ever since among politicians of agrarian and Populistic tradition. Populist agitators used the ethnic symbols more or less indiscriminately, British along with Jewish, though some of them bore down with peculiar viciousness on the Semitic symbol. As the new critics have pointed out, certain Eastern intellectuals of the patrician sort, such as Henry and Brooks Adams and Henry Cabot Lodge, shared the Populist suspicion and disdain of the plutocracy and likewise shared their rhetorical anti-Semitism. John Higham has called attention to a third anti-Semitic group of the nineties, the poorer classes in urban centers. Their prejudice cannot be described as merely verbal and rhetorical. Populists were not responsible for a protest signed by fourteen Jewish societies in 1899 that

"no Jew can go on the street without exposing himself to the danger of being pitilessly beaten." That happened in Brooklyn, and the mob of 1902 that injured some two hundred people, mostly Jewish, went into action in Lower East Side New York.

* * *

Two other aspects of identification between the old Populism and the New Radical Right require critical modification. Talcott Parsons, Max Lerner, and Victor Ferkiss, among others, find that the old regional strongholds of Populism tended to become the strongholds of isolationism in the period between the two world wars and believe there is more than a fortuitous connection between a regional proneness to Populism and isolationism. These and other critics believe also that they discern a logical connection between a regional addiction to Populism in the old days and to McCarthyism in recent times.

In both of these hypotheses the critics have neglected to take into account the experience of the South and mistakenly assumed a strong Populist heritage in the Middle West. Although one of the strongest centers of Populism, if not the strongest, the South in the foreign policy crisis before the Second World War was the least isolationist and the most internationalist and interventionist part of the country. After the war, according to Nathan Glazer and Seymour Lipset, who base their statement on opinion poll studies, "the South was the most anti-McCarthy section of the country." It is perfectly possible that in rejecting isolationism and McCarthyism the South was "right" for the "wrong" reasons, traditional and historical reasons. V. O. Key has suggested that among the reasons for its position on foreign policy were centuries of dependence on world trade, the absence of any concentration of Irish or Germanic population, and the predominantly British origin of the white population. Any adequate explanation of the South's rejection of McCarthy would be complex, but part of it might be the region's peculiarly rich historical experience and with its own assortment of demagogues — Populistic and other varieties — and the consequent acquirement of some degree of sophistication and some minimal standards of decency in the arts of demagoguery. No one has attempted to explain the South's anti-isolationism and anti-McCarthyism by reference to its Populist heritage — and certainly no such explanation is advanced here.

To do justice to the new critique of Populism it should be acknowledged that much of its bill of indictment is justified. It is true that the Populists were a provincial lot and that much of their thinking was provincial. It is true that they took refuge in the agrarian myth, that they denied the commercial character of agricultural enterprise and sometimes dreamed of a Golden Age. In their economic thought they overemphasized the importance of money and oversimplified the nature of their problems by claiming a harmony of interest between farmer and labor, by dividing the world into "producers" and "nonproducers," by reducing all conflict to "just two sides," and by thinking that too many ills and too many remedies of the world were purely legislative. Undoubtedly many of them were fascinated with the notion of conspiracy and advanced conspiratorial theories of history, and some of them were given to apocalyptic premonitions of direful portent.

To place these characteristics in perspective, however, one should enquire how many of them are peculiar to the Populists and how many are shared by the classes, or groups, or regions, or by the period to which the Populists belong. The great majority of Populists were provincial, ill-educated, and rural, but so were the great majority of Americans in the nineties, Republicans and Democrats as well. They were heir to all the superstition, folklore, and prejudice that is the heritage of the ill-informed. The Populists utilized and institutionalized some of this, but so did their opponents. There were a good many conspiratorial theories, economic nostrums, and oversimplifications adrift in the latter part of the nineteenth century, and the Populists had no monopoly of them. They did overemphasize the importance of money, but scarcely more so than did their opponents, the Gold Bugs. The preoccupation with monetary reforms and remedies was a characteristic of the period rather than a peculiarity of the Populists. The genuine Populist, moreover, was more concerned with the "primacy of credit" than with the "primacy of money," and his insistence that the federal government was the only agency powerful enough to provide a solution for the agricultural credit problem proved to be sound. So did his contention that the banking system was stacked against his interest and that reform in this field was overdue.

The Populist doctrine of a harmony of interest between farmer and labor, between workers and small businessmen, and the alignment of these "producers" against the parasitic "nonproducers" is not without precedent in our political history. Any party that aspires to gain power in America must strive for a coalition of conflicting interest groups. The Populist effort was no more irrational in this respect than was the Whig coalition and many others, including the New Deal.

The political crises of the nineties evoked hysterical responses and apocalyptic delusions in more than one quarter. Excesses of the leaders of a protest movement of provincial, unlettered, and angry farmers are actually more excusable and understandable than the rather similar responses of the spokesmen of the educated, successful, and privileged classes of the urban East. There would seem to be less excuse for hysteria and conspiratorial obsessions among the latter. One thinks of the *Nation* describing the Sherman Silver Purchase Act as a "socialistic contrivance of gigantic proportions," of J. Laurence Laughlin writing of "the great silver conspiracy" in the *Atlantic Monthly* of 1896, or of Police Commissioner Theodore Roosevelt declaring in "the greatest soberness" that the Populists were "plotting a social revolution and the subversion of the American Republic" and proposing to make an example of twelve of their leaders by "shooting them dead" against a wall. There was Joseph H. Choate before the Supreme Court pronouncing the income tax "the beginnings of socialism and communism" and "the destruction of the Constitution itself." For violence of rhetoric *Harper's Weekly*, the *Atlantic Monthly*, the New York *Tribune*, and the Springfield *Republican* could hold their own with the wool-hat press in the campaign of 1896. Hysteria was not confined to mugwump intellectuals with status problems. Mark Hanna told an assembly of his wealthy friends at the Union League Club they were acting like "a lot of scared hens."

Anarchism was almost as much a conspiracy symbol for conservatives as Wall Street was for the Populists, and conservatives responded to any waving of the symbol even more irrationally, for there was less reality in the menace of anarchism for capitalism. John Hay had a vituperative address called "The Platform of Anarchy" that he used in the campaign of 1896. The Springfield *Republican* called Bryan "the exaltation of anarchy"; Dr. Lyman Abbott labeled Bryanites "the anarchists of the Northwest," and Dr. Charles H. Parkhurst was excited about the menace of "anarchism" in the Democratic platform. It was the Populist sympathizer, Governor John Peter Altgeld of Illinois, who pardoned the three anarchists of Haymarket, victims of conservative hysteria, and who partly corrected the gross miscarriage of justice that had resulted in the hanging of four others. The New York *Times* promptly denounced Governor Altgeld as a secret anarchist himself, and Theodore Roosevelt said that Altgeld would conspire to inaugurate "a red government of lawlessness and dishonesty as fantastic and vicious as the Paris Commune." There was more than a touch of conspiratorial ideology in the desperate conservative reaction to the agrarian revolt. An intensive study of the nineties can hardly fail to leave the impression that this decade had rather more than its share of zaniness and crankiness and that these qualities were manifested in the higher and middling as well as the lower orders of American society.

Venturing beyond the 1890's and speaking of populists with a small "p," some of the new critics would suggest that popular protest movements of the populistic style throughout our history have suffered from a peculiar addiction to scares, scapegoats, and conspiratorial notions. It is true that such movements tend to attract the less sophisticated, the people who are likely to succumb to cranks and the appeal of their menaces, and conspiratorial obsessions. But before one accepts this as a populistic or radical peculiarity, one should recall that the Jacobin Scare of the 1790's was a Federalist crusade and that the populistic elements of that era were its victims and not its perpetrators. One should remember also that A. Mitchell Palmer and the superpatriots who staged the Great Red Scare of 1919–1920 were not populistic in their outlook. One of the most successful conspiratorial theories of history in American politics was the "Great Slave Conspiracy" notion advanced by the abolitionists and later incorporated in the Republican party credo for several decades.

Richard Hofstadter has put his finger on a neglected tendency of some Populists and Progressives as well, the tendency he calls "deconversion from reform to reaction," the tendency to turn cranky, illiberal, and sour. This happened with disturbing frequency among leaders as well as followers of Populism. Perhaps the classic example is the Georgia Populist, Tom Watson, twice his party's candidate for President and once for Vice President. When Watson soured he went the whole way. By no means all of the Populist leaders turned sour, and there has been an overemphasis on a handful of stock examples, but there are several valid instances. Even more disturbing is the same tendency to turn sour among the old Populist rank and file, to take off after race phobias, religious hatreds, and witch hunts. The reasons for this retrograde tendency among reformers to embrace the forces they have spent years in fighting have not been sufficiently investigated. It may be that in some instances the reform movement appeals to personalities with unstable psychological traits. In the case of the Populists, however, it would seem that a very large part of the explanation lies in embittered frustration — repeated and tormenting frustration of both the leaders and the led. . . .

In his study of populist traits in American society, Edward Shils has some perceptive observations on the difficult relations between politicians and intellectuals. He adds a rather wistful footnote:

How painful the American situation looked to our intellectuals when they thought of Great Britain. There the cream of the graduates of the two ancient universities entered the civil service by examinations which were delightfully archaic and which had no trace of spoils patronage about them. . . . Politics, radical politics, conducted in a seemly fashion by the learned and reflective was wonderful. It was an ideal condition which was regretfully recognized as impossible to reproduce in the United States.

He himself points out many of the reasons why this is possible in Britain, the most dignified member of the parliamentary fraternity: respect for "betters," mutual trust within the ruling classes, deferential attitudes of working class and middle class, the aura of aristocracy and monarchy that still suffuses the institutions of a government no longer aristocratic, the retention of the status and the symbols of hierarchy despite economic leveling. No wonder that from some points of view "the British system seemed an intellectual's paradise."

America has it worse — or at least different. The deferential attitude lingers only in the South, and there mainly as a quaint gesture of habit. Respect for "betters" is un-American. Glaring publicity places mutual trust as the *modus vivendi* among the political elite. No aura of aristocratic decorum and hierarchal sanctity surrounds our governmental institutions, even the most august of them. Neither Supreme Court nor State Department nor Army is immune from popular assault and the rude hand of suspicion. The sense of institutional identity is weak, and so are institutional loyalties. Avenues between the seats of learning and the seas of power are often blocked by mistrust and mutual embarrassment.

America has no reason to expect that it could bring off a social revolution without a breach of decorum or the public peace, nor that the revolutionary party would eventually be led by a graduate of exclusive Winchester and Oxford. American politics are not ordinarily "conducted in a seemly fashion by the learned and reflective." Such success as we have enjoyed in this respect — the instances of the Sage of Monticello and the aristocrat of Hyde Park come to mind — have to be accounted for by a large element of luck. Close investigation of popular upheavals of protest and reform in the political history of the United States has increasingly revealed of late that they have all had their seamy side and their share of the irrational, the zany, and the retrograde. A few of the more successful movements have borrowed historical reputability from the memory of the worthies who led them, but others have not been so fortunate either in their leaders or their historians.

One must expect and even hope that there will be future upheavals to shock the seats of power and privilege and furnish the periodic therapy that seems necessary to the health of our democracy. But one cannot expect them to be any more decorous or seemly or rational than their predecessors. One can reasonably hope, however, that they will not all fall under the sway of the Huey Longs and Father Coughlins who will be ready to take charge. Nor need they, if the tradition is maintained which enabled a Henry George to place himself at the vanguard of the antimonopoly movement in his day, which encouraged a Henry Demarest Lloyd to labor valiantly to shape the course of Populism, or which prompted an Upton Sinclair to try to make sense of a rag-tag-and-bob-tail aberration in California.

For the tradition to endure, for the way to remain open, however, the intellectual must not be alienated from the sources of revolt. It was one of the glories of the New Deal that it won the support of the intellectual and one of the tragedies of Populism that it did not. The intellectual must resist the impulse to identify all the irrational and evil forces he detests with such movements because some of them, or the aftermath or epigone of some of them, have proved so utterly repulsive. He will learn all he can from the new criticism about the irrational and illiberal side of Populism and other reform movements, but he cannot afford to repudiate the heritage.

III. POPULISM AT THE CROSSROADS: THE CAMPAIGN OF 1896

Matthew Josephson: FREE SILVER AS "THE COWBIRD" OF THE REFORM MOVEMENT

In the following excerpt Matthew Josephson, a popular historian, presents the traditional opinion that the Populist Party was betrayed by opportunists in the Campaign of 1896.

WILLIAM BRYAN of Nebraska, the poor country-town lawyer, had for eight years been carving out a career in politics after an old American pattern. The mind of this born elocutionist, in the view of William Allen White, who knew him, may well have been stuffed with the spirit of old steel engravings such as covered the walls of his library in Lincoln, Nebraska — engravings of Jefferson, Jackson, Lincoln, Webster, and above all, of Henry Clay, "towering almost ten feet high in foreground, badly out of perspective, pleading with the lilliputian senators — all in stocks and tail coats . . . all dignified and serious, wrapped in improving mediation. . . . Bryan all his life seemed to draw from this picture his fine Fourth Reader views . . . of life." It may have been true likewise, as others felt, that Bryan was: "Not really able nor even clear headed, lacking capacity as a thinker"; that his abstinence from drink and tobacco, his religious piety and ill-concealed evangelism, made him a little "the humbug" to hardened professional colleagues, upon whom he too must depend in the last resort.

Yet Bryan's very "simplicity" led him to embrace historic opportunities which the wise old men of the East could not, or would rather not, see. In his campaigns, in his lecture tours on behalf of the American Bimetallic League, he saw with his own eyes the force stirring at the "grass roots" of the republic. Then his evangelism, his single-minded fanaticism, like Cromwell's, was suited to the revolutionary times, and lent point and astonishing force to his speech.

On the other hand, by his own convictions Bryan was far from being the "dangerous revolutionary" whom his frightened adversaries pictured. The limits of his protest (like the limitations of his thought) were well defined, and became more evident later as his career extended itself prosaically, after the glamour, the excitation, the intoxicated rhetoric of his great hours in 1896 had passed. He mourned at the bier of the pure-hearted Lyman Trumbull, but differed strongly with the old war Republican's later socialistic views. He flirted successfully with the Populists in Nebraska and won their co-operation in his creditable, though unsuccessful, fight for the United States Senatorship in 1894. Ignatius Donnelly of Minnesota said of him: "We put him to school, and he wound up by stealing the schoolbooks." He worked with the Populists, they believed him one

From *The Politicos*, copyright, 1938, 1966, by Matthew Josephson, pp. 669–79, 681–84. Reprinted by permission of Harcourt, Brace & World, Inc.

of them; yet he was not of them.

The Populists, the radical wing of the farmers of the Middle Border, were bent on reversing the old Jacksonian and libertarian doctrines, which had sought free land, freedom from governmental or authoritarian restrictions, and now sought rather increased national government support to guarantee their old liberties. They clamored for a "paternalistic" Federal ownership of monopolies in railroads and grain elevators, for the extension of government Treasury facilities in farm credits and warehousing. Monetary inflation was but incidental, a means to an end of sweeping and rational reform. Here Bryan did not follow where they led. On these radical demands he was vague or silent.

It was the singular role of this "evangelist and crusader, with a great musical, vibrant voice, fashioned for political purposes," to check the impetus of the Farmers' Alliance (Populist) movement, divert its logical drive for genuine land reform, and shift the objective of the land uprising to the monetary issue solely. Glozing over the laborious reforms demanded by the agrarian radicals, this young Christian Statesman led his followers to the social impasse of monetary inflation, from which he promised them untold benefit — above all, a longed-for redistribution of wealth — would certainly flow.

Bryan, finally, saw no harm in carrying on an opportunistic collaboration with the Silver and Copper Barons, feeling sincerely that attainment of their objectives would aid his own people too. Such a compromise was perfectly typical of the Puritan temperament. The aggressive mining interests that worked behind the scenes, according to some observers, seriously considered Bryan as the most likely figure for the plan of a "stampede,"

whose outcome none as yet could foretell. For Bryan, though less known than the older politicians, attracted the Populists, and might provide the best bridge leading to fusion with their important voting strength. "Bryan is a Populist in all but the name," one of the agrarian leaders wrote to Weaver, in the early spring of 1896. He proposed that Bryan should head the Populist and Democratic tickets both.

While without modesty about his ambitions, there was something meek and patient as well as practical in the way in which Bryan advanced his cause. His humility avoided enmities. Numerous politicians and delegates recalled afterward that Bryan spoke to them seriously in asking their support at the 1896 convention; although, as Champ Clark afterward said, he seemed to be the only one who believed in his chances. But hopefully he persisted, like other Favorite Sons, in reaching as many people as he could, holding himself the most available "regular" Democrat from a "doubtful" Northern State, and destined to be chosen by elimination. Bryan and his wife wrote thousands of letters to leaders and members of State Organizations concerning platform resolutions, pledges, and the support of his own incredible candidacy. "I perhaps was personally acquainted with more delegates than any other man who was mentioned as a candidate," Bryan observed.

Carefully the young man wheeled himself into position to be struck by presidential lightning. He was delighted when he contrived to appear in the momentous debate over the silver plank, serving as one of the "keynoters" of the Western silver uprising within the party. It was a further stroke of luck that he was the last speaker for the silver faction, and was given additional time in return for augmented speaking time asked by the opposing Gold Democrats — Hill, Vilas, and Russell. Bryan's speech was long prepared, woven from old strands of ideas and phrases used in lectures throughout the South and the Mississippi Valley.

As he waited for his hour, a friend, Clark Howell, editor of the Atlanta *Constitution,* sent him a note scribbled on an envelope: "This is a great opportunity." Bryan, according to his own recollections, wrote in reply: "You will not be disappointed," and sent the envelope back.

Though the external behavior of the "revolutionary mob" which overran the Chicago convention may have been enough to frighten the Eastern Democrats, inwardly the convention's action reflected order and a firm command. Altgeld, its directing spirit, though a semi-invalid, sat quietly in his place among the delegates, always holding himself impassive, as under an iron control.

On Tuesday, July 7, the recommendation of the party's national committee — which traditionally was followed — that Senator David B. Hill act as "temporary chairman," that is, preside over the proceedings of the nominating convention, was voted down uproariously by a majority of 556 to 349, John W. Daniel, of Virginia, an ardent bimetallist, receiving the office. It was the opening blow and a finishing stroke: "the sceptre of political power passed from the strong, certain hands of the East to the feverish, headstrong mob of the West and South." The too crafty Hill was like a man who was out of his element.

On the following day the credentials of the Nebraska prosilver delegates, Bryan at their head, were passed upon, and with the Territorial delegates a two-thirds majority was achieved for Free Silver, and the obstructive power of the minority eliminated.

While the convention, waiting for further business, gave itself over to celebrating the overthrow of the Goldbugs, Altgeld was called by tremendous, sustained ovations to make an impromptu speech. In a brief, vigorous statement, he set the keynote: "no compromise" in the party resolutions. "With his sharply chiselled French Revolution face, his high, ringing voice, his bitter vehemence of manner, and his facility for epithet," as a hostile journalist described him, Altgeld figured largely in the horrific myth of a bogeyman which gripped all the conservative classes. He was pictured as

. . . the most dangerous influence in the convention [having] the stamp of the agitator who, when the bludgeon had failed of its full work, would be ready with the poisoned knife, and who, in leading a victory-drunken mob, would not hesitate to follow pillage with the torch.

Yet the vast majority of the audience applauded to the echo their hero who might have had the nomination if he had been eligible. It was the music of consoling vindication for Altgeld.

Thursday, July 9, which began with the reading of the platform by Senator J. K. Jones on behalf of the Resolutions Committee, saw the climax of the convention. By its platform the new Democratic Party which was being born took the unprecedented step of disavowing the ruling national Administration of its own President. Mr. Cleveland was denounced in so many plain words for making private contracts for bond sales to the Morgan banking syndicate and increasing the national debt in time of peace; he was condemned for his high-handed use of the court injunction and Federal troops; more, the august "House of Lords," our Supreme Court, for its recent decisions was also visited with the party's disapproval. Then the silver plank was read before listeners, tense, bitter or jubilant:

We are unalterably opposed to monometallism, which has locked fast the prosperity of an industrial people in the paralysis of hard times. . . . We demand the free and unlimited coinage of both silver and gold at the present legal ratio of 16 to 1, without waiting for the aid or consent of any other nation.

There was to be no compromise. Pitchfork Ben Tillman, as arranged, began the debate upon the platform resolutions with a fierce castigation of the President, in a style which recalled plainly the secessionist days of 1860. The men of the South, he cried, were up in arms against their exploiters:

We of the South have burned our bridges behind us so far as the Eastern Democrats are concerned. . . . We denounce the Administration of President Cleveland as undemocratic and tyrannical. . . . A plutocratic despotism is sought to be established.

In answer, Hill of New York rose to the defense of his old rival, Cleveland, and spoke also for the minority opposing Free Silver coinage. With his usual smacking emphasis upon the word "Democrat" he began:

I am a Democrat, but I am not a revolutionist. My mission here to-day is to unite, not to divide — to build up, not to destroy. . . . My friends, I speak more in sorrow than in anger. You know what this platform means to the East. . . . We want the principles of Jefferson and Jackson. We want no greenback currency. . . . We want no paper currency.

Hill, the most conciliatory speaker for the Gold Democracy, was little heard by the tempestuous men of the Chicago convention. Even less Senator Vilas, of Wisconsin, Cleveland's former Postmaster General, though he gave warning of a bloody debacle to come: "Perhaps somewhere in this country there lurks a Robespierre, a Danton, a Marat?" Nor did the delegates and the spectators, by turns turbulent, hostile, or bored, give heed to the sickly Governor Russell of Massachusetts, who, after pleading in a weak voice against repudiation, exclaimed finally that "our country, if not this convention, will listen to our protest."

Bryan of Nebraska now strode toward the platform "two steps at a time." He had the bearing of "a strong-limbed, strong-lunged" athlete as he stood for an instant facing "the wild crowd. . . . It had been known for hours that the convention might be stampeded for the Nebraskan. . . . Ear-splitting noises were heard; waves of scarlet fans danced in the galleries." The whole convention, the moment, demanded impatiently a voice to express its purpose, its hope. Bryan had himself marvelously well in hand, as he relates, having been thoroughly prepared since the night before; in his mind was the epopee of the "cross of gold" which he had been saving for such an occasion, "recognizing its fitness for the conclusion of a climax." Many of those who were present also attest to the "miracle" of the young speaker's mastery over the crowd, as we remember the enchantment of a great actor in our youth. With a gesture he silenced the long roar of applause that had greeted him; the clear, soaring voice began its work.

His opening words were as modest as they were courteous. He was not so "presumptuous" as to measure himself against the more distinguished gentlemen who preceded him; but, he cried:

The humblest citizen in all the land, when clad in the armor of a righteous cause, is stronger than all the hosts of error. I come to speak to you in defense of a cause as holy as the cause of liberty — the cause of humanity.

He passed over the bitter personal issues raised by the reigning President. "The individual is but an atom; he is born, he acts, he dies; but principles are eternal; and this has been a contest over a principle." Thus Bryan, "with . . . the zeal which inspired the crusaders who followed Peter the Hermit," clothed the interests of the silver Democrats in the noblest ideology.

In the face of so much legend that the sense of Bryan's appeal was "socialistic," we must note the precise line of his reasoning, even at the emotional crest of his oratory. In its essence it reflects not a landless, toolless proletarian opposition, but the mentality and social relationships of the lower middle class, the numerous body of smallholders, artisans, country lawyers, and shopkeepers at crossroads to whom Bryan belonged and whom he would lead in a crusade against the *big* property-holders and *big* capitalists. Thus with a significant and deeply characteristic stroke of dialectics — paradoxical and fallacious at once — he defined the businessman anew in a passage which he was proud of and inserted at the last moment as the only new material among his old silver arguments. The Eastern Democrats had accused the silver men of "disturbing business," and Bryan, turning to the gold delegates, said:

. . . . we reply that you have disturbed our business interests by your course. We say to you that you have made the definition of a business man too limited in its application. The man who is employed for wages is as much a business man as his employer, the attorney in a country town is as much a business man as the corporation counsel in a great metropolis; the merchant at the crossroads store is as much a business man as the merchant of New York; the farmer who goes forth in the morning and toils all day — who begins in the spring and toils all summer — and who by the application of brain and muscle to the natural resources of the country creates wealth, is as much a business man as the man who goes upon the board of trade and bets upon the price of grain; the miners who go down a thousand feet into the earth . . . and bring forth from their hiding places the precious metals to be poured into the channels of trade are as much business men as the few financial magnates who, in a back room, corner the money of the world. We come to speak for this broader class of business men.

With a reasoning familiar to our own ago also, Bryan drew a line of cleavage between the small or petit-bourgeois capitalist and the great finance capitalists of the world money centers. In such argument, as in such a "revolution," there is confusion and contradiction, just as there is latent discord, jealousy, and sectional hostility among the conglomeration which forms the party of the middle class, the landed interests and producing interests, fused by an hour of crisis and opportunity. Thus, unlike Bebel in Germany and Jaurès in France, rational economic doctrinaires who were at this time directing the Social Democratic movement of the working class in Europe, Bryan addressed himself to numerous divisions and groups in the body politic, offering something to each. For the producing and toiling masses he seems to attack the ruling financial class, and proposes a redistribution of wealth, saying:

There are those who believe that, if you will only legislate to make the well-to-do prosperous, their prosperity will leak through on those below. The Democratic idea, however, has been that if you legislate to make the masses prosperous, their prosperity will find its way up through every class which rests upon them.

But repeatedly he turns to his dominant theme, the defense and exaltation of the landed interest; he apotheosizes the frontiersman, the pioneer. Once more Jefferson's "chosen" people and Jackson's "embattled farmers" are fighting for cheaper money and relief from their debts. He extols

. . . the hardy pioneers who have braved all the dangers of the wilderness, who have made the desert to blossom as the rose — the pioneers away out there (pointing to the West), who rear their children near to Nature's heart, where they can mingle their voices with the voices of the birds — out there where they have erected schoolhouses for the education of their young, churches where they praise their Creator, and cemeteries where rest the ashes of their dead — these people, we say, are as deserving of the consideration of our party as any people in the country. It is for these that we speak. . . . Our war is not a war of conquest; we are fighting in the defense of our homes, our families, and prosperity.

It is significant how he passes over in the most general terms concrete issues of tariff, of statism, of the regulation of monopolies, raised by the truly radical farm leaders, while harping on the theme of cheap money.

Did the great cities favor the gold standard? But the great cities themselves

. . . rest upon our broad and fertile prairies. Burn down your cities and leave our farms, and your cities will spring up again as if by

magic; but destroy our farms and the grass will grow in the streets of every city in the country.

As the measured words of the orator rolled over the great hall the tense crowd responded rhythmically with crashes of applause to the points brought home. At one climax, Bryan's voice rose, and he gesticulated in graceful pattern:

We have petitioned, and our petitions have been scorned; we have entreated, and our entreaties have been disregarded; we have begged, and they have mocked when our calamity came. We beg no longer; we entreat no more; we petition no more. [A dramatic pause.] *We defy them.*

The last words, "We defy them!" were flung out with a most impressive movement of the speaker's whole body; they rang with an accent of "superb disdain," and were followed by an outburst of mad cheering from 20,000 throats. Then amid renewed silence, in more subdued but intense accents, Bryan launched into the famous conclusion of his speech, whose meaning has been much overlooked, closing with an appeal to patriotism in the face of the traditional enemy, England. The mixed sectional-class conflict was given a memorable nationalistic or jingo hue. Must we wait for England to decree bimetallism in the world before we moved, he asked? It was the "issue of 1776" again.

If they dare to come out in the open . . . we will fight them to the uttermost. Having behind us the producing masses of this nation and the world, supported by the commercial interests, the laboring interests, and the toilers everywhere, we will answer their demand for a gold standard by saying to them: *You shall not press down upon the brow of labor this crown of thorns, you shall not crucify mankind upon a cross of gold.*

The hall awoke from its hypnotic silence in a bedlam of cheering and parading which lasted for half an hour. The Goldbugs were undone. The Western Democracy had found its leader. The various State delegations forming in processions gathered before the Nebraska section and dipped their flags before the Nebraska standard. Only the Eastern gold men sat sullen before this largely spontaneous uproar, and in the vote upon the platform which followed cast their minority ballots in a dying opposition. According to the conservative press of New York and Chicago, it was a "political debauch," an "orgy," likened to the opening of the Reign of Terror in Paris. "Hell was broken loose in Chicago," Wickham Stead cabled to London.

Other more discriminating observers noted the unusual enthusiasm and spontaneity which marked this convention, an unfamiliar phenomenon at our popular political gatherings, and utterly absent at the preceding Republican convention at St. Louis. One wrote, in London:

It was essentially the most genuine and impromptu political movement that has been known for many a decade. It was really the birth of a new party — a party devoted in spirit, whatever its mistakes of method, to human rights and human progress, to the welfare of the common people, to the promulgation of a newer and truer Democracy.

Bryan of Nebraska — his words had been flashed throughout the country by telegraph, making a profound or a terrifying impression — had introduced a new spirit into the formal contests of the parties, evoked a national, quasi-revolutionary impulse on behalf of silver-money inflation of a scope which few men, least of all the rather shifty mine operators who originally sponsored silver coinage, could have calculated in advance. The little-known Western politician, by the "miracle" of his speech, was as a consequence to be catapulted into the presidential nomination and an electoral contest which would shake the very foundation stones of the republic. Bryan might have been nominated by acclamation at the moment his speech ended; but the balloting which was to follow the adoption of the silver platform was held over until the next day.

"Bryan, Bryan! No crown of thorns, no cross of gold!" The paraders and revelers sang.

Bryan, whose candidacy had been "amusing" on the morning before July 10, was second only to Bland in the first three ballots and assumed the lead on the fourth. Another adjournment, and a hasty conference was called by the leaders and wirepullers; then on the fifth ballot the "break" came, and a majority was won by the Boy Orator and "tribune of the people." On the following day the press significantly reported:

The Democratic National Convention nominated William J. Bryan of Nebraska for President. . . . Withdrawals . . . brought the gold reserve . . . below $100,000,000.

A man of wealth, Arthur Sewall, a banker, shipbuilder, and railway director who happened to believe in Free Silver, was then named as the vice-presidential candidate.

The hysterical crowds who came to his hotel carried the Nebraskan upon their shoulders and called for a speech. "My friends," he responded, "I feel this is going to be a campaign of sentiment. This is to be a fight for the common good."

* * *

The decision taken at the People's Party convention at St. Louis, in mid-

July, seemed but to augment the alarming class-sectional character of the struggle this year. To St. Louis also the agents of the silver cabal quickly repaired, bent as they had been for two years on achieving fusion between the Populists and the Democrats. This is Marcus Daily, and to allied Silverite politicians like Senators Stewart, Jones of Nevada, and Pettigrew, as to the veteran People's Party leaders, Weaver, Allen, and Sockless Jerry Simpson, would break the bonds between the rural West and the financial Northeast, and with it the hegemony of the Eastern Goldbugs.

These men now contrived to manage the Populist convention by means of wirepulling as effective as any party assembly ever saw. Henry Demarest Lloyd in a letter of the time reflected on how curious it was that "the new party, the Reform party, the People's party, should be more boss-ridden, gang-ruled, gang-gangrened than the two old parties of monopoly." But yesterday this well-meaning reformer had joined the Populists with enthusiasm and worked to bring about a coalition between farmers and union labor, convinced that "the people are about to take possession of the property of the people." Today bitter doubts assailed him.

The veteran Populist and Farmers' Alliance organizers were now within sight of victory, power, and office, after so many years of wandering in the wilderness. Did they not have the substance of what they wanted in Bryan? asked Simpson of Kansas. Bryan was a Populist in all but name, and what did the party name matter?

Amid scenes of emotional storm usually attending the farmers' party conventions, while the highly extroverted Mary Elizabeth Lease nearly burst a blood vessel, and the chairman burst his galluses out of sheer excitement, Senator Allen, the "incorruptible" Weaver, and other leaders steered the convention toward fusion, despite a stubborn opposing minority. This consisted in part of clear-sighted prolabor radicals such as Lloyd, in part of the idealistic Southern Populists who had faced prejudice and violence in their efforts to erect a truly progressive third-party organization, free from Southern Bourbonism and official corruption. (It was becoming really a second "white man's party" in a region devoted to the single-party system.)

"By the time this money question is settled," argued Senator Marion Butler of North Carolina, . . . the great transportation question — that great question which stands side by side with the money question — will be upon you." The problems of transportation, the trusts and monopolies — these were what the People's Party had come into existence to fight, he urged.

Other opponents of fusion felt that the moment was a turning-point in their young party, which had grown in a few years to 1,500,000 votes and dominated a half-dozen Western and Southwestern States. Would it not be the "death knell" of their movement, they asked, if they were swallowed up in the Democracy?

The People's Party, as we have remarked, had risen as a "peasants' party" of the Middle Border and the South, advocating carefully studied land reforms, popular credit institutions and co-operative marketing measures, which at the period represented a realistic view of their problems. Slowly, despite special difficulties, it approached coalition with trade-union groups and even socialists of various colors. Must whatever gains in educational and cohesive force the persistence of their Organization promised be now jeopardized, gambled away by the opportunists who cried with Weaver and Allen *"Win this time"?*

The minority stoutly urged a course defined in an unfortunate phrase: to stick to "the middle of the road," that is, drive between the two big parties. But the answer from Allen carried the day:

Do you want . . . a President who is in favor of . . . Government ownership of railroads and telegraphs?

I do not want [my constituents] to say to me that the Populists have been advocates of reforms, when they could not be accomplished, but when the first ray of light appeared and the people were looking with expectancy and anxiety for relief, the party was not equal to the occasion; that it was stupid; it was blind; it kept "in the middle of the road" and missed the golden opportunity.

Weaver for his part welcomed the "new Pentecost," and would not refuse the proffered assistance of 3,000,000 Silver Democrats and 1,000,000 Silver Republicans "simply because they have shown the good sense to come with an organized army ready for battle." Bryan was a champion of the people. Let us go to the rescue of this gallant knight, "assailed . . . by the sleuth hounds of the money power of the world," he exhorted.

At the last moment, after having agreed to nominate Bryan of Nebraska by acclamation, the veteran Populists gagged at approving of Sewall, the banker and railroad man, for the Vice-Presidency. The fire-eating Thomas Watson of Georgia was proposed instead. A tense contest was fought over this issue, in the midst of which came a somewhat chivalrous telegram from Bryan, refusing the Populists nomination if his running mate were not also named by them. But

this dispatch was highhandedly withheld from the convention by Senator Allen, and the Populists, in ignorance, proceeded to name Bryan and Watson for their ticket.

In their platform, too, the Populists showed radical deviations from the Democrats, demanding besides free and unlimited coinage of silver the establishment of postal savings bank, direct election of Senators and of Presidents and Vice-Presidents, the initiative and referendum, government ownership of public utilities, and Federal public-works expenditure for the unemployed. In this anomalous manner they responded to the "bugle call" of fusion, amid frenzied demonstrations, singing, and waving of the American flag.

Lloyd, a bitter observer of the last minute proceedings, wrote on July 18, 1896:

The poor people are throwing up their hats in the air for those who promise "to lead them out of the wilderness" by way of the currency route. . . . The people are to be kept wandering forty years in the currency labyrinth, as they have for the last forty years been led up and down the tariff hill.

He reflected further that this "fortuitous collection of the dissatisfied" lacked all grasp of any fundamental principle which might keep a genuine party movement together:

The Free Silver movement is a fake. Free Silver is the cow-bird of the Reform movement. It waited until the nest had been built by the sacrifices and labour of others, and then it laid its eggs in it. . . . The People's party has been betrayed. . . . No party that does not lead its leaders will ever succeed.

Robert F. Durden: A REAPPRAISAL OF "THE COWBIRD THESIS"

The traditional conception of Populist politics in 1896 has recently been challenged by Robert F. Durden. Drawing upon new manuscript sources, Durden contends that because the old antipathy toward Populist fusion with the Democrats rested largely on hostile testimony, it was, in fact, untenable.

MANY STUDIES have been made of the election of 1896, but confusion and error persist concerning the role of the Populists, and several important questions about their activities remain unanswered, or have been answered incorrectly. . . .

Basic to any understanding of national policies in 1896 is the currency question. In early October of that year Henry Demarest Lloyd called "Free silver . . . the cow-bird of the Reform movement. It waited until the nest had been built by the sacrifices and labour of others, and then it laid its eggs in it, pushing out the others which lie smashed on the ground." Many historians have quoted and endorsed Lloyd's interpretation, which is subjective and misleading. Lloyd was a socialist committed to government ownership of the means of production and distribution and had joined the People's party to try to unite industrial workers and agrarians under its banner and to lead the Populists to a gradual acceptance of socialism. Although the Populists had incorporated a demand for government ownership of railroads and telegraphs in their Omaha platform of 1892, neither they nor the Farmers' Alliance members were doctrinaire socialists — they were, rather, angry agrarian capitalists who found themselves unprotected by government from

exploitation by the railroads. They responded with a pragmatic proposal for government ownership, and though many were made uncomfortable by the request it died out only when federal regulation became a meaningful reality in the twentieth century.

Lloyd, on the other hand, advocated government ownership as a step in the establishment of a different economic and social order. But even in Illinois his efforts to secure endorsement of this demand (Plank 10) were defeated in early 1894, and Lloyd was denounced by Herman E. Taubeneck, chairman of the Populist national committee. Taubeneck spoke both for the agrarians and for some of the urban workers when he greeted Lloyd's collectivist proposal with the declaration that if "this is what you came to the people's party for, we don't want you. Go back from where you came with your socialism.". . .

Tom Watson of Georgia, perhaps the best known figure among the "radical" Populists of the South, spoke for the bulk of his party late in 1895 when he vowed that he would go no farther toward "Socialism and Radicalism" than the Georgia Populists had gone. That group, Watson reported to Marion Butler [Populist Senator from North Carolina], had given the "cold shoulder" even to the doctrines of Jacob S. Coxey of Ohio and had adopted

From Robert F. Durden, "The 'Cow-Bird' Grounded: The Populist Nomination of Bryan and Tom Watson in 1896," *Mississippi Valley Historical Review*, Vol. L (December 1963), pp. 397–423. Reprinted by permission of the Organization of American Historians.

the "most conservative" platform that the party had ever had. Watson urged that he, Butler, and others who favored a moderate course should begin to use their newspapers to educate public sentiment and thus make it impossible for extremists to control the forthcoming national convention. That important gathering would need a chairman who "has nerve enough to rule with a rod of iron those hot-headed recalcitrants who want to load us down with extreme-isms." Prophetically, and ironically in view of subsequent developments, Watson thought that William V. Allen, Populist senator from Nebraska — or Marion Butler himself — would be a good man to wield the "rod of iron" against the extremists.

Too much should not be made of Watson's comments to Butler. Serious differences of ideology and strategy existed even among the anti-socialist Populists, but to most Populists of the period *socialism* was the real, late-coming "cow-bird" that tried to capture the nest. . . .

The Populists had discovered in the campaign of 1892 that the silver plank had the greatest popular appeal of any of their numerous demands. True, a majority of the Populists were not willing to eliminate proposals for other important reforms, but Populist leaders were no different from those of the older parties in yielding to the drift of the voters' opinions. Benjamin O. Flower, editor of *The Arena,* one of the few national magazines supporting Populism and reform in general, advised Marion Butler late in 1894 that wise action by the Populists would bring them victory in 1896. Flower wanted the Populists to continue to educate the people on all lines of reform but especially to emphasize the money question now that Cleveland had brought to a climax a life-and-death struggle between the "money power" and

the people. "No more class legislation, more money and less misery" would be the winning slogan according to Flower.

Butler needed no urging. As the acknowledged leader of the Populists in North Carolina and president of the national Farmers' Alliance, he had clearly demonstrated the capacity for adroit political leadership that the third party much needed and often lacked. No matter how just a reform might be, Butler argued, for a political party to make a leading issue of it before the people were ready would be folly. With all his power he hoped to help make the financial question "the one overshadowing issue in the next great struggle between the classes and the masses."

Unlike some of the western Populists, Butler disapproved obliterating other demands in order to add emphasis to the silver issue. He admitted that government ownership of the railways was not widely popular but insisted that no great reform was ever popular at first. He thought that the correct solution of the railway problem was almost as important as that of the financial question. But the depression and money shortage had awakened the public to the silver issue and made the time ripe "for concentrating under one banner" those who favored reform. After winning the silver victory, Butler concluded, "I shall favor making a war to the finish on the greedy, grasping, private monopolies, which to-day are using and abusing the great functions of government that should be owned by the people and used by the people."

In short, what Butler and many other third-party leaders across the nation thought they had found by 1894–1895 was the common denominator essential to the life of a major political party in the United States. State and sectional groupings that differed widely because of history, economic interests, and geography might, with the lucky denominator, join together to win the "first victory." Doctrinaires and dogmatists to the contrary, most of the Populist leaders viewed this "first victory" as the preliminary to many others that would culminate in a national victory gained in a campaign based on the financial issue. . . .

Two minority factions within the People's party, for quite different reasons, expressed misgivings about the silver-first strategy and the constant calling for cooperative action of all the friends of silver. The socialist followers of Lloyd, while numerically small and unrepresentative, derived their significance from the brilliance and literary skill of Lloyd himself. The other minority was much larger and consisted principally of Populists in the South, especially the deep South, who, for sectional or local reasons, disliked the idea of any cooperation between Populists and Democrats. Since real Republican organizations scarcely existed in some of these southern states, Populists there had to contend with the high-handed and often dishonest machinations of the long-entrenched Democrats. Not for silver, or for that matter any other essentially national issue, were these Populists willing to blur the distinction between themselves and the Democrats. Opposing all fusion on principle, they styled themselves "middle-of-the-road" Populists.

The first signs of the uneasiness of the midroaders in 1896 came in connection with selecting the time for the Populists' national convention. To hold their meeting before either of the other two parties would lessen the chances of cooperation or fusion, or cause the fusion, if any, to take place strictly on Populist terms with Populist candidates. The Populist national committee met in St. Louis on

January 17 to decide when and where the convention would be held. The Republican committee had scheduled their convention for St. Louis, June 17, and on January 16 the Democratic national committee decided to hold their meeting in Chicago on July 7.

Butler favored a late convention, as did most of the national leaders of the party. The Populist state chairman of Nebraska as early as August, 1895, had urged that the national convention be held after both old parties had "unquestionably turned their backs upon the white metal." On the other hand, a Populist national committeeman from Thomson, Georgia (Watson's home town), sent Butler his proxy with regrets that he could not be in St. Louis and expressed the hope that the committee would call for an early spring convention to meet in some southern city, preferably Atlanta. The Populist national committee, apparently reflecting the sentiment of the majority of the party, decided to hold the convention in St. Louis on July 22 and invited all opponents of the two old parties to cooperate with the Populists. . . .

The Republican convention that opened on June 16 declared itself "unreservedly for sound money" and opposed to the free coinage of silver "except by international agreement with the leading commercial nations of the earth, which agreement we pledge ourselves to promote. . . ." The Republicans also equivocated on their candidate by naming William McKinley of Ohio, who had in the past been friendly to silver. Senator Teller of Colorado, Senator Richard F. Pettigrew of South Dakota, and other silver Republicans from the far West bolted the party and announced the organization of the Silver Republican party. The plan of the Silver Republicans and the Populist leaders was to rally around Teller as the ideal candidate for the united silver forces. The Coloradan had favored the income tax and a few other reform causes and had stood for years as one of the most widely respected spokesmen for silver. If the eastern friends of the Cleveland administration had the votes to force a compromise candidate on the Democratic convention, true silver Democrats by the thousands would come to the silver banner that would be primarily the property of the Populists. If, on the other hand, the admittedly powerful silver wing of the Democracy should be in control sufficiently to name the candidate as well as as to write the platform, no candidate would be as acceptable as Teller, according to the Silver Republican and Populist leaders, if the silver Democrats were sincere about wanting to unite all silver forces. . . .

But a veritable revolution had occurred in the Democratic party; its full extent could not be measured until the fervent silverites began to flock into Chicago for the convention on July 7. "The Democratic movement toward silver in the last six months before the Chicago convention," Allan Nevins writes, "was like an avalanche: a mere whisper at first, then a half-imperceptible shift in the landscape, and suddenly a roar, a crash, an irresistible cataclysm.". . .

On the day the convention opened, Altgeld's public statement doubting that Teller could carry Illinois was a major setback for the Teller boom. Taubeneck's announcement that the Populists would not support Representative Richard P. Bland of Missouri or Governor Horace Boies of Iowa was one factor that worked against those two leading contenders for the nomination. This situation together with Bryan's careful pre-convention work

for support among the delegates, his outstanding record in Congress as an able friend of reform, his clear record of friendliness to and cooperation with the Populists in his home state, and, lastly, his magnetic qualities as displayed in his famed address to the convention led to the young Nebraskan's nomination by the Democrats.

Not only had the Democrats named the most exciting and dynamic presidential candidate in well over a generation, but the platform, in addition to the call for free silver and other financial reforms, bore the stamp of Altgeld in its denunciation of Cleveland's action in the Pullman boycott and of "government by injunction as a new and highly dangerous form of oppression. . . ." Too often remembered only for its assaults on the "anti-American," "British policy" of gold monometallism, the platform also demanded stricter federal regulation of the railways, an end to national banknotes, a tariff for revenue only (after the money question was settled), an income tax, the protection of American labor by prevention of the "importation of foreign pauper labor," stricter enforcement of antitrust legislation, and various other reforms. For all the Populists who since the birth of the party had cried "principle above party," a cruel moment of decision had arrived.

National history made it clear by 1896 that an important third party faced one of two fates: it disappeared after growing strong enough to force one of the major parties to embrace its ideas and the bulk of its membership, or, given the right set of circumstances, it might become in a time of general party disintegration and chaos one of the two major parties. The Democrats in 1896, however, did not equivocate and dodge in the face of an overwhelming national question as the Whigs had tried to do in the decade before the Civil War. Although no Populist planned or wished the party's death, the western Populists could accept this national fate for their party with equanimity and a redoubled resolve to work for Bryan, silver, and then other reforms. Since Populists in many western states had already cooperated or "fused" with Democrats in local and state battles against Republicans, the absorption of the People's party on the national scene by the Bryan Democracy seemed natural enough.

To most of the southern Populists, on the other hand, absorption by the Democrats was not within the realm of reason. No matter what the historic pattern concerning third parties or the logic of the national situation might be, sectional exigencies in the South demanded the preservation of a separate and distinct Populist party. The situation that faced the Populists after the Democratic convention seemed to be this: if the Populists did not fall in line behind Bryan and free silver, the bulk of the western strength of the party would be lost as Populists there left the party to march under the Democratic banner of reform; if the Populists did embrace Bryan, southern Populists to save their local political lives — and largely for sectional reasons — would be sorely tempted to bolt the the national Populist party. Either way, in the short period between the conclusion of the Democratic convention and the opening of the Populist meeting in St. Louis on July 22, the split between the pro-Bryan Populists and the southern midroaders seemed to augur the certain dissolution of the People's party. . . .

Since Populist response even to the name "Democrat" differed greatly according to sectional circumstances, confusion and anxiety mounted as the Populists began to converge on St. Louis. Reporters found that some delegates, too poor to pay railway fares, had walked long distances to reach the convention; some were forced to sleep in the parks in order to afford the "nickel-lunch." Heat gripped the city. Eastern newsmen, like their publishers and editors, were intolerant of the desperate farmers: "The crazy people who fancy that some one is always sneaking paris green into their chowder or needles into their hash are not more suspicious than this body of 1,400 more or less 'touched' would-be rulers of the country."

Butler refused interviews and kept quiet as he had said he would, but few other Populist leaders chose that course. Reuben F. Kolb, prominent leader of the Alabama delegation, declared strongly for Bryan: "I am willing to make the fight on one plank, so long as it is monetary reform. That is the paramount issue. I'm a middle-of-the-road Populist, but I've got sense enough to walk around a mud hole." From Texas, where anti-Bryan and midroad sentiment was strongest, a delegate asserted that a straight Populist ticket would be named because "Texas is goin to run this Convention and dictate the nominations." Although Tom Watson had chosen not to attend the convention, he had dispatched the Georgia delegation with instructions to stand by the full Populist platform and fight fusion. At the other extreme from Watson and the Texans, Representative Jerry Simpson of Kansas told the large and generally approving Kansas delegation that the "issue is paramount, and men dare not play politics at such a time as this. If this Convention should refuse to indorse Bryan the Populist party would not contain a corporal's guard in November."

Out of this babel a plan emerged. The

party made nominations and was largely held together. Leadership, bold and imaginative as the difficult situation required, played a key role. The fundamental fact was that most Populists wanted free silver as the first step and symbol of overdue reforms. Most Populists wanted also to maintain the Populist party organization intact for the national purpose of keeping the Democrats "honest" and out of the Clevelandites' hands and for various local purposes that differed according to geography and circumstance. Lloyd's widely accepted charge that the Populist leaders at St. Louis "tricked and bulldozed and betrayed" as they carried out a conspiracy to destroy Populism is not only untrue but also ignores the dilemma that faced the party.

No one knows who first suggested that the Populists should nominate Bryan, reject the Democrats' vice-presidential nominee, Arthur Sewall of Maine, and put up their own candidate for the vice-presidency. Contemporary accounts make clear that Butler early and energetically identified himself with this plan for saving the party and the silver cause. As unprecedented and fraught with difficulty as the plan was, it apparently grew out of the complexities that the executive committeemen found when they gathered in St. Louis on Sunday evening, July 19; the plan was ultimately accepted by the great majority of both the leaders and the ordinary delegates who filled the hotel lobbies with noisy, often angry debate.

Butler arrived with the reputation of being a midroader. He continued to be a moderate one in the sense that he, Taubeneck, Ignatius Donnelly, William A. Peffer, and others in the majority agreed that the national organization of the Populist party should neither be destroyed by a bolt of extreme fusionists or

extreme midroaders from the convention nor be eliminated by being absorbed in the Democracy. This sentiment the executive committee established at its first meeting. Senator James K. Jones of Arkansas, the Democratic national chairman, and Governor William J. Stone, Democrat of Missouri, met with the Populist leaders and insisted on full endorsement of the Democratic ticket or nothing. Bryan's spokesmen emphatically rejected, as did the western Populists, the idea of Butler and others for an independent Populist ticket with Populist candidates, to be followed by fusion with the other silver groups on the electoral ticket according to the proportionate strength of the various parties in each state. One alleged spokesman for Bryan, Matt Ward of Omaha, declared flatly that, "This talk about dividing electors will not be allowed; it can't go. I have Mr. Bryan's ultimatum in my pocket, and will deliver it to the Populists at the proper time."

Butler had discovered, even before arriving in St. Louis, that while it was both difficult and impolitic to attack Bryan himself, the same was not true of the Democratic vice-presidential nominee. Arthur Sewall was a well-to-do president of a national bank and director of railway and other corporations, who happened to believe in free silver; he was nominated because he was from Maine and would furnish geographical balance for a ticket headed by a Nebraskan. Any hope that his eastern "respectability" would help hold irate Clevelandites in the party proved groundless.

The most enthusiastic Democrat knew that Bryan had about the same chance in New England as McKinley had in the deep South. The extremist minority of midroad Populists, who were ready to split the party rather than accept Bryan, joined with the more moderate leaders who searched for a way to save the party and the silver cause in announcing that Sewall could never be accepted by the Populists. Capitalizing on this anti-Sewall feeling, Butler conferred again with Senator Jones on Monday, July 20, and proposed, according to press accounts which seem reliable, that the Populists endorse Bryan if the Democrats would drop Sewall and accept the Populist nominee for vice-president. When Jones refused to listen to this proposal, Butler reportedly became angry and assailed the Democrats for "wanting the earth." Butler's later statement to newsmen revealed little other than his hope for a way out: "Some seem to think that there is a danger of a split, but there will be none. The different elements will put their heads together and agree on a plan of action. . . ."

Just as Jones rebuffed Butler, Weaver and other spokesmen for the complete Bryan-Sewall ticket rejected the same proposition when James H. ("Cyclone") Davis of Texas and Donnelly presented it on behalf of the Populist executive committee. Any attempt to displace Sewall, according to Jones and his allies, would lead to irreconcilable complications and place both parties in a ridiculous attitude. "The committee," Jones declared, "must be as loyal to the vice-presidential nominee as to the presidential candidate."

Regardless of Jones's refusal to talk about a sacrifice of Sewall, a key group of Populist leaders, including Marion Butler, had decided by Tuesday, July 21, that the exigencies of the situation called for the nomination of Bryan and a southern Populist on a Populist ticket backed by a Populist platform. But this program would have to be fought for in open convention, where a slight misstep might see minorities on either extreme uniting to thwart what seemed to be the complicated preference of the majority. When the Populist national committee met on July 21, the executive committee recommended and secured Butler's nomination as the temporary chairman and keynote speaker of the convention. Although Davis and Weaver had been frequently mentioned by their respective factions for the temporary chairmanship, opposition to Butler was slight both in the meeting of the national committee and in the convention itself.

The convention that finally opened on Wednesday, July 22, consisted of almost 1,400 hot, confused, and tense delegates. Palmetto fans agitated the still air, and audibility of the speakers on the platform was so poor that a big-voiced delegate from Wisconsin was used as a "repeater." A few women and Negro delegates were scattered about the hall. Each state was allowed one delegate for every senator and representative it had in Congress and additional delegates in proportion to the Populist vote cast in the state. This plan of representation meant that New York had only forty-four delegates, while Texas and North Carolina each had about a hundred votes, and Kansas, with the largest western delegation, had eighty-two. One analysis of the convention by sections showed that the South had approximately six hundred delegates; the East, one hundred and fifty; the North (including Ohio and the states to the Missouri River except for Missouri and the Dakotas), two-hundred and forty; and the West (beyond the Missouri), three hundred and fifty-six.

With extremists on both sides waiting for their openings to yell in uninhibited Populist style, thirty-three-year-old Butler successfully walked an oratorical tightrope in his keynote address. He suggested that the Democrats, from a mixture of alarm and conscience, had committed "petty and grand larceny by stealing the People's party platform almost in its entirety." What then should the Populists do? They should be consistent in their insistence upon putting issues above partisanship and help settle the financial question so that other fundamental matters could be dealt with next.

But the separate People's party was still absolutely necessary; without it "the next Democratic National Convention would repudiate the platform it recently adopted at Chicago, and Mr. Bryan would stand no more chance four years hence of being nominated by that party than Thomas Jefferson would if he were alive." Without alluding directly to the plan for a southern vice-presidential nominee, Butler concluded with a plea for unity, which, under the circumstances, was scarcely mere rhetoric. A party that had raised up a great principle and split the two old parties, he argued, "is not going to be foolish enough to allow itself to split on methods and detail. We will stand together."

After the keynote address the convention adjourned until evening in order to give the committee on permanent organization time to prepare its report. Since there had been no floor fight about Butler's election, all hands readied for battle over the election of the permanent chairman. The extreme midroaders filled the air with their threats of bolting if the leaders tried to force the nomination of Bryan; the election of the permanent chairman, as all admitted, would be the first test of the power of the various factions. . . .

The majority report of the committee on permanent organization recommended as permanent chairman Senator Allen of Nebraska, a fervent supporter of Bryan

who was also believed by most observers to favor Sewall. The minority report named James E. Campion of Maine, an extreme midroader. Allen was chosen, 758 to 564.

Thus a majority of the convention agreed on a Bryan man for permanent chairman; an even larger majority later accepted the report of the committee on the platform as made by Weaver and rejected proposals backed by some of the extremists led by Coxey. The platform recognized the financial question as the "great and pressing issue" before the country, and Populists invited the "cooperation of all organizations and citizens" who agreed on "this vital question.". . .

The undecided, crucial question remained: would the extreme midroaders bolt, as they constantly threatened, after the majority named Bryan as the Populist candidate? The extreme fusionists, who insisted that the Populists had to accept Sewall as well as Bryan, were counting on either a stampede to Sewall in the enthusiastic aftermath of Bryan's nomination or an adjournment after that nomination to give them time to woo a majority to Sewall. If the southern extremists bolted, the task of selling Sewall to the delegates remaining in the convention and the party would become that much easier.

In order to prevent any possibility of Sewall's being nominated, the minority report of the committee on rules and procedures called for a reversal of the usual order of nominations and the naming of the vice-presidential candidate first. Texans, Georgians, and others rallied to this idea, not only because they were anti-Sewall but also because they hoped that somehow the presidential nomination might be miraculously saved for a Populist. The next round of voting began. North Carolina, which had divided its ninety-five votes equally in the Allen-Campion contest, was a key state in the tense fight on the order of business. At the proper time in the roll call, Representative Harry Skinner mounted a chair and shouted:

"North Carolina stands with Nebraska. When we came here this morning we were for the minority report, but since then we have had assurances from Kansas, Nebraska, and other . . . States that, if we would permit the regular order to prevail the cause of Populism in the South should be recognized by the nomination of a Southern candidate for Vice-President. North Carolina therefore casts 85 votes for the majority report and 10 for the minority."

As the roll call neared the end, rumors began to circulate that the Bryanites had narrowly won. Southern midroaders rushed to beg the North Carolina delegation to change its vote. Skinner hurriedly consulted with Butler, rushed back to his delegation, and again mounted the chair:

"Mr. Chairman, North Carolina cast its vote to nominate a President first, after pledges from Kansas and other States that afterwards a [Southern] Populist should be nominated for Vice-President. Are you sincere? I demand to know as I am empowered to change the vote of North Carolina."

Bedlam descended upon the convention as cries of "yes, yes" and "no" filled the air. Thomas Patterson, head of the Colorado delegation and a supporter of the Bryan-Sewall ticket, yelled that it was "disgraceful that in a convention like this any such deals should be mentioned." He vowed that "Colorado had no part in it." Skinner, probably exhausting the patience of many with his further remarks about a southern man deserving

the vice-presidential nomination, concluded by casting all of North Carolina's 95 votes for the minority report. With the convention again in churning commotion and Marion Butler cheering "as long as his voice held out," Allen finally restored order to announce that the minority report had carried by 785 votes to 615. A Populist vice-presidential candidate would be named first.

The midroaders — extremists and moderates cooperating — had won their first clear victory. They celebrated accordingly, with the extremists temporarily ignoring the limited nature of their victory. The anti-Bryan midroaders hurt their own cause through lack of organization and noisy immoderation in general. Despite these handicaps, the midroaders came into their own at about sixteen minutes before 1:00 A.M. (the appropriateness of the "sixteen to one" amused them) on Saturday, July 25, when one of their best-loved spokesmen, Tom Watson of Georgia, received the Populist nomination for the vice-presidency. . . .

Just why Watson, with his long record of strong opposition to fusion of any kind, had consented to play a vital role in a plan designed to bring about quasi-fusion of the Populists and Democrats is a puzzle that may never be solved. Perhaps the best answer is the one that he himself gave shortly after the convention. "I will accept the nomination," he explained, in "the interest of harmony and to prevent disruption of the [P]opulist party, which seemed imminent." Watson added that under the circumstances he fully endorsed the convention's action; furthermore, when he and Bryan had been in the House of Representatives they had "voted together on every measure. . . ." He subsequently explained that he had been sincere in saying earlier that he would not accept either place on the straight Populist ticket that he advocated, and he continued: "I stayed away from the Convention partly to avoid prominence, and the Georgia delegation had positive instructions not to allow the use of my name. . . . When I said I would not accept I did not dream that such a crisis could possibly come upon our party."

In thinking that his candidacy was necessary to "harmonize the factions and save the party," Watson was correct. Although he was not the only southern Populist who could have served the purpose, he was well qualified, except for an erratic streak that was destined to cause much difficulty in the campaign. . . .

The early-morning nomination of Watson brought the Populists to the last and in many ways most delicate phase of their convention, the nomination of the presidential candidate. It was delicate because the extreme fusionists had continually argued that the nomination of Bryan without Sewall was impossible and that Bryan would not, indeed could not, accept any such nomination. Could the Populists nominate him even if he asked that they not do so? Many delegates were impatient for the answer to that question as the celebration following Watson's nomination began to die down in the hall; some had come to the evening session with their luggage in tow. But it was about 1:00 A.M. (Saturday, July 25), the end of a long day of exciting developments, and Weaver's motion for adjournment was declared carried amid confusion and shouts of "no."

The telegraph, even before the newspapers, kept Bryan in Lincoln fully informed of developments at the Populist convention. Jones had advised him, however, to ignore all embarrassing questions and let his well-known record speak for itself. But when the Populists voted to nominate their vice-presidential candidate first, the Democratic national chairman telegraphed Bryan the news, asked him what should be done if Sewall were not nominated by the Populists, and advised him that in that event he (Jones) favored declining a nomination by the Populists. Bryan responded, before or about the time that the Populists were making their speeches naming the various vice-presidential nominees, that he agreed with Jones and wished his name withdrawn from consideration if Sewall were not also nominated. These telegrams were in the hands of Thomas Patterson of Colorado that evening. The St. Louis newspapers, as well as most other daily papers carried either the texts or the substance of the telegrams on Saturday, July 25, 1896. In other words, every Populist who attended the last crucial session of the convention on that Saturday had read in the morning newspapers or had otherwise heard that Bryan did not wish to be nominated by the Populists unless Sewall was also chosen. Yet the overwhelming majority of the Populists nominated the Nebraskan as their candidate for the presidency of the United States.

They were not tricked into this action. They did it because they had to do it for the survival of the People's party and for an excellent fighting chance to win the reforms they and many others desired. The Populist leaders were gambling, for they did not know what Bryan would do; but, being politicians, they knew that candidates never go out of their way to reject votes. In his speech nominating Bryan, Weaver first established clearly that he too had been won over to the program of Butler and the other moderate midroaders. Then he went straight to the embarrassing news from Nebraska:

"You have all read the papers this morning; you have all read the manly dispatch from . . . Bryan. No man could have done less and be a man. . . . But . . . this question has reached a point where neither Mr. Bryan nor his personal friends have any right whatever to say what the action of this convention shall be. This is a greater question than the personality of its candidates."

James G. Field of Virginia, the vice-presidential candidate of the Populists' "blue-gray" team in 1892, seconded Bryan's nomination and moved that it be made unanimous. Although Allen was at first inclined to rule the motion in order, angry cries from the extreme midroaders led to a hasty huddle of the leaders on the platform and the decision to proceed with the roll call of States. Six more hours of oratory and nominations followed. The extremists rallied behind S. F. Norton of Illinois, Populist editor and author of one of the numerous books dealing with the money question. The balloting resulted in 1,042 votes for Bryan, 340 for Norton. After the tradi-

tional parade of the state banners and noisy celebration, which Josephus Daniels found about as enthusiastic as the scene he had witnessed when the Democrats named Bryan in Chicago, the exhausted Populists prepared to leave St. Louis.

Such a struggle as the Populists had waged at St. Louis left serious divisions in the party. Yet the important fact is that the great majority of the party and its leaders had held together for Bryan and national reforms. The campaign ahead posed difficult problems for both the Populists and Bryan, who ultimately accepted his nomination in a gracious manner. Tom Watson, as subsequent events showed, had allowed himself to be badly miscast in the political drama. But under the leadership of Marion Butler, whom the Populist national committee elected as national chairman at the conclusion of the convention, the bulk of the Populists fought as best they could for Bryan and financial reform. Free silver, far from being a "cow-bird," had swept the Populists into an important role in the epochal campaign of 1896.

Suggestions for Additional Reading

In addition to John D. Hicks's book the most important general progressive works on Populism and its antecedents include Solon J. Buck, *The Granger Movement: A Study of Agricultural Organization and Its Political, Economic and Social Manifestations, 1870–1880* (Cambridge, Mass., 1913) and *The Agrarian Crusade: A Chronicle of the Farmer in Politics* (New Haven, 1920); and Fred A. Shannon, *The Farmer's Last Frontier: Agriculture, 1860–1897* (New York, 1945).

Richard Hofstadter's *The Age of Reform* is only one of many recent studies by revisionists. Other representative treatments of Populism or the Populist mentality (there is a tendency among revisionists to use the term rather imprecisely) are to be found in Daniel Bell (ed.), *The New American Right* (New York, 1955); Edward A. Shils, *The Torment of Secrecy* (Glencoe, Ill., 1956); and Victor Ferkiss, "Populist Influences on American Fascism," *Western Political Quarterly*, X (June 1957), pp. 350–373. Besides the antirevisionist selections presented in this anthology, the most significant work is Norman Pollack, *The Populist Response to Industrial America: Midwestern Populist Thought* (Cambridge, Mass., 1962). *Agricultural History*, XXXIX (April 1965) offers an interesting symposium by revisionists and critics: Norman Pollack, "Fear of Man: Populism, Authoritarianism, and the Historians," pp. 59–67; Oscar Handlin, "Reconsidering the Populists," pp. 68–74; Irwin Unger, "Critique of Norman Pollack's 'Fear of Man,'" pp. 75–80; and J. Rogers Hollingsworth, "Commentary — Populism: The Problem of Rhetoric and Reality," pp. 81–85.

The overwhelming majority of regional and state histories dealing with Populism, like Walter Nugent's Kansas study have been written from a progressive viewpoint. Regional studies include Russel B. Nye, *Midwestern Progressive Politics: A Historical Study of Its Origins and Development, 1870–1958* (Ann Arbor, 1959); C. Vann Woodward, *Origins of the New South, 1877–1913* (Baton Rouge, 1951); and Theodore Saloutos, *Farmer Movements in the South, 1865–1933* (Berkeley, 1960). State studies include Alex M. Arnett, *The Populist Movement in Georgia: A View of the "Agrarian Crusade" in the Light of Solid-South Politics* (New York, 1922); John B. Clark, *Populism in Alabama* (Auburn, 1927); Marion Harrington, *The Populist Movement in Oregon, 1889–1896* (Eugene, 1940); Roscoe C. Martin, *The People's Party in Texas: A Study in Third Party Politics* (Austin, 1933); William DuB. Sheldon, *Populism in the Old Dominion: Virginia Farm Politics, 1885–1900* (Princeton, 1935); and Francis B. Simkins, *The Tillman Movement in South Carolina* (Durham, N. C., 1926). An exception to the predominantly progressive character of such studies is *The Agrarian Movement in North Dakota* (Baltimore, 1925) by Paul R. Fossum, an economist of conservative leanings.

Biographies of Populist or near-Populist leaders are important historical sources. Among the most important are: Chester McA. Destler, *Henry Demarest Lloyd and the Empire of Reform* (Philadelphia, 1963); Paolo E. Coletta, *William Jennings Bryan, Vol. I: Political Evangelist, 1860–1908* (Lincoln, 1964); Fred E. Haynes, *James Baird Weaver* (Iowa City, 1919); Stuart Noblin, *Leonidas LaFayette Polk, Agrarian Crusader*

90

(Chapel Hill, 1949); Martin Ridge, *Ignatius Donnelly: The Portrait of a Politician* (Chicago, 1962); Francis B. Simkins, *Pitchfork Ben Tillman, South Carolinian* (Baton Rouge, 1944); and C. Vann Woodward, *Tom Watson, Agrarian Rebel* (New York, 1938).

Several recent studies are directly relevant to understanding the Populist Party in the larger context of the political history of the era: Robert F. Durden, *The Climax of Populism: The Election of 1896* (Lexington, Ky., 1965); Paul W. Glad, *McKinley, Bryan, and the People* (Philadelphia, 1964); J. Rogers Hollingsworth, *The Whirligig of Politics: The Democracy of Cleveland and Bryan* (Chicago, 1963); and Stanley L. Jones, *The Presidential Election of 1896* (Madison, 1964).